Preac...
in the In... ...

TRANSITIONAL LEADERSHIP
IN THE LATINO/A CHURCH

Efrain Agosto

JUDSON PRESS
PUBLISHERS SINCE 1824
VALLEY FORGE, PA

Interior design by Wendy Ronga, Hampton Design Group.
Cover design by Lisa Delgado, Delgado and Company, Inc.

Names: Agosto, Efrain, author. Title: Preaching in the interim : transitional leadership in the Latino/a church/Efrain Agosto.
Description: Valley Forge, PA: Judson Press, [2018]. Identifiers: LCCN 2018011441 (print) | LCCN 2018028102 (ebook) | ISBN 9780817081867 (epub) | ISBN 9780817017958 (pbk.: alk. paper) Subjects: LCSH: Church work with Hispanic Americans. | Interim clergy. | Change—Religious aspects—Christianity. | Preaching to Hispanic Americans. | Church year sermons. | Hispanic Americans—Religion. Classification: LCC BV4468.2.H57 (ebook) | LCC BV4468.2.H57 A36 2018 (print) | DDC 252/.061—dc23
LC record available at https://lccn.loc.gov/2018011441

Printed in the U.S.A.
First printing, 2018.

I dedicate this book to the leaders and members of
La Segunda Iglesia Bautista de Nueva York.

Thank you for your service and dedication
to the cause of Christ
in the historic community
of East Harlem
for so many years.

¡A Dios sea la Gloria!

Contents

Preface
A Latino/a Church in Manhattan

I was born and raised in New York City. In fact, I was born in the Bronx, raised in Brooklyn (my family moved there when I was nine years old), studied in Manhattan (for my undergraduate degree), and married in Queens (at my wife, Olga's, church). This pretty much covers the city, except for Staten Island. I think I have been there just twice in my life. Nonetheless, I was a thoroughgoing New Yorker for the first twenty-four years of my life. However, seminary and graduate work and my first full-time job in ministry took us to New England for some thirty years (first Boston, then Hartford). I did not return to work in my hometown until 2011, when I took a position as professor of New Testament studies at New York Theological Seminary. This reconnected me to New York City and its ministers and churches, as well as to students in training for such ministries. Two years into my work in urban theological education for New York area ministers in training, a Latino/a Baptist church in the historic Latino/a neighborhood of East Harlem called me to be their interim pastor for eight months.

I had worked in East Harlem in my first job after college during the late 1970s before going to seminary in the Boston area. I remembered it as a mostly Puerto Rican community that had its first Latino/a families, and churches, as far back as the 1920s. In fact, the church I was called to serve had been established in 1928! During my tenure as interim pastor, they celebrated their eighty-fifth anniversary (in October 2013). However, this was not unusual as East Harlem churches go. I was called to serve *Second* Spanish Baptist Church of New York. So there was a *First*, founded a few years earlier in that decade. Latino/a Baptists, along with Latino/a Presbyterians, Methodists, and a little later, Pentecostals, had been establishing churches in East Harlem and beyond for decades since the 1920s.

Over the years, I had met valued colleagues in ministry who had been reared as Latino/a Baptists and still served in those churches and denominations, namely, as members of American Baptist Churches USA. Among these were Orlando Costas and his protégés Elizabeth Conde-Frazier, Loida Martell-Otero, and brothers Luis and Danny Cortes. The latter three, all currently clergy in the Philadelphia area (except in the case of Dr. Martell-Otero, a professor at Philadephia's Palmer Seminary until her recent appointment as dean at Lexington Theological Seminary in Kentucky), had been reared in the Second Spanish Baptist Church. One of the deacons at Second Baptist (known best by their Spanish nickname, "La Segunda") was the mother of the Cortes brothers, Mrs. Miriam Cortes.

Dr. Elizabeth Conde-Frazier, a seminary professor and now college dean, and I went to high school together in Brooklyn, and she was raised in the Central Baptist Church of Brooklyn. She used to tell me stories of the historic Latino/a Baptist clergy and churches in New York City. Now I, reared as a Latino Pentecostal (Assemblies of God) in Brooklyn, found myself pastoring, for a season, one of those historic ABCUSA Latino/a churches in Metro New York. The Rev. Dr. Isaac J. Casteñada, Associate Regional Minister of ABC Metro New York, had approached me in early 2013 about serving as Interim Minister at La Segunda, and given all these previous connections to the church, even though I had never been there, I was intrigued, we explored, and they called. This book of sermons is a result of my time with this historic church.

Acknowledgments

There are many people who made this book possible. Beginning at the beginning, I would like to thank the Rev. Dr. Isaac Castañeda, Associate Regional Minister for the American Baptist Churches of Metropolitan New York, who first approached me about the possibility of serving in interim ministry at Second Spanish Baptist Church of New York in East Harlem. He did so carefully, by first having me preach at an all-city ABC-Hispanic Good Friday Service on March 29, 2013, which was held that year at La Segunda. Then I met with the church leaders and preached one more time before they extended a formal invitation. Thank you, Isaac, for your wise leadership.

After I completed those wonderful eight months, I had about twenty-five written sermons, the most I have ever had in one church series! It was my dear friend, the Rev. Dr. Elizabeth Conde-Frazier, a published author with Judson Press, who suggested I approach her terrific editor, Rebecca Irwin-Diehl, about the possibility of publishing those sermons in a book that would include descriptions of my experience of serving a historic Latino/a church in interim ministry. Rebecca enthusiastically encouraged me to submit a book proposal, and once accepted, she expertly shepherded me through the process of collecting the sermons, editing them, and preparing the manuscript. Thank you, Rebecca, as well as your editorial colleagues at Judson Press, Lisa Blair and Laura Weller, for your kindness, patience, and expertise in helping me produce this book and making it, despite my shortcomings and slowness as a writer and editor, a better volume than it would have been without you.

Acknowledgments

New York Theological Seminary, my place of full-time employment since July 2011, including during the period of my part-time service at Second Baptist Church in 2013, afforded me not one, but two sabbaticals that included time to begin this project (Spring 2014) and complete it (Fall 2017). Thank you, President Dale Irvin, Dean Kirk Cohall, and faculty colleagues, for supporting and encouraging my efforts in this and other publication projects during those two timely sabbaticals. I also want to offer a word of great appreciation for my NYTS Work Study Student in the Academic Year 2016–2017, Alicia Viera, who helped me with the translations of these sermons from Spanish to English, as I prepared them for publication. Thank you, Alicia, for your skillful and thoughtful attention to these sermons in their original form.

My eight months as interim minister at Second Baptist Church included a lot of car travel. Although the church graciously provided a terrific apartment in the top floor of the church, which I used happily and liberally, I spend a lot of time on the road between my job in the Upper Westside of Manhattan, my home in West Hartford, Connecticut, and the church in East Harlem. I want to thank Olga Gisela, my wonderful spouse, who often traveled with me to the church on weekends and who, with her warm personality, endeared herself to the members of the church for the short time we were there. Thank you, Gisela, for your love and support, and for the many ways in which you showed better pastoral sensitivities than I.

And, of course, there are the leaders and members of La Segunda Iglesia Bautista de Nueva York. As you will see throughout these sermons, they are a faithful, committed community. A special word of thanks to deacons, trustees, and other church leaders, including Wilfredo Acevedo, Miriam Cortes, Viterba Ortiz, Juanita Aviles, Jose Marrero, and Luis Gandia, who worked so closely with me as together we shepherded the church through those interim months, while you continued to look for your permanent pastor. It was an honor to serve with you and everyone whose name I cannot specifically mention in these brief comments. It is to that historic church, its legacy, its people, as well as the surrounding community of East Harlem that I dedicate this book. Amen!

Introduction

Sermons of an Interim

This book presents the sermons I preached at Second Spanish Baptist Church of New York for eight months, beginning with Good Friday and Easter services, and continuing with a series of sermons on church life as experienced by the apostle Paul's Philippian Christians. During a summer series on the Book of Acts, I continued with the topic of the nature of the church and its leadership. Then I turned in the fall to the importance of Christian education, history, and thanksgiving for Latinx[1] churches in transition. The interim period concluded with Advent, Christmas, and New Year's sermons as I tried to prepare the church for the next stage of its search for permanent pastoral leadership.

In presenting this book of sermons, my purpose is multifaceted. First, I hope the reader will be interested in this slice of life of a twenty-first-century Latino/a church through the perspective of an interim minister's sermons, particularly how one such pastor mounted a preaching program for a relatively brief season of service. Second, my hope is that the biblical reflections and particular cultural references in these sermons will remind the reader of the rich theological and cultural heritage present in US Latino/a churches and of what we can learn from such experiences and history. Finally, I hope to celebrate the challenges and struggles, hopes and possibilities of the Latinx church in the United States, as exemplified in this one slice of church life and by how one preaches in such a setting.

I am most grateful to the leaders, members, and participants of Second Spanish Baptist Church of New York, "La Segunda," and for the opportunity to be part of their lives for this brief period of such a long, storied history.

Note

1. The terms to describe US *Latinidad* in the twentieth and twenty-first centuries have changed over the years, from the naming of specific groups—Puerto Rican, Cuban, Dominican, Mexican American, Latin American, etc.—to the US Census Bureau's arbitrarily lumping together those of all backgrounds under "Hispanic" beginning in the 1980s, to more politically attuned "Latino" and "Latina" or "Latino/a," sometimes in reaction against the Census Bureau's use of "Hispanic." *Latinx* is the most recently emerging term, especially among the academic community, acknowledging the various sexualities inherent in our community. I mostly use "Latino/a" in this book of sermons, reflecting my initial preaching in 2013, unless of course I am referring to a specific group, such as Puerto Ricans.

Part One

The Nature of Church Ministry in Paul's Letter to the Philippians

In this first part of this book of sermons, I share some of the sermons I preached at the beginning of my official tenure as interim pastor at Second Spanish Baptist Church in New York. I decided that I would preach through an entire Pauline letter, both because of my academic expertise with the apostle Paul's letter to the Philippians in particular and because the idea of presenting the life of an early Christian church, as known through its founder's pastoral letter to them, appealed to me.

Thus I used the example of Paul's experience with the church at Philippi to offer a series of sermons that I thought could help this Latino/a church in transition with regard to the nature of church ministry, including thanksgiving and love (Philippians 1:3-11), the example of Christ's service for our ministry and leadership today (2:1-30), and the qualities of other leadership exemplars from the early church, namely, Paul, Timothy, and Epaphroditus (2:12-30). I concluded the series with two sermons on the importance of setting goals as a church (3:12-16) and doing our work for God and the church with care and excellence (4:4-9).

Throughout this series, I reminded Second Baptist that in Paul's ministry with the churches, we learn from him and them the basic Christian values of *koinonia* (community and partnership), *agapē* (love), *dokimazō* (approval and discernment), *diakonia* (service), *telios* (goal setting), and *aretē* (excellence).

1
Gratitude and Love in the Church

Philippians 1:3-11
Sermon preached on April 7, 2013

> I thank my God every time I remember you, constantly praying with joy in every one of my prayers for all of you, because of your sharing in the gospel from the first day until now. I am confident of this, that the one who began a good work among you will bring it to completion by the day of Jesus Christ.—Philippians 1:3-6

I give thanks to God for the opportunity to serve in the coming months as your interim pastor. Let me explain by way of introduction that I was born in the Bronx and raised in Brooklyn; my parents came from Puerto Rico in 1950. I studied all my life in New York City until I entered a theological seminary near Boston, Massachusetts, in 1979. Since that time, my wife, Olga, and I (we married in 1983) have lived and ministered in New England—Boston and Hartford—along with our two children, Joel and Jasmin, now young adults in their late twenties. I thank God for these experiences that have prepared us for this moment to be in ministry with all of you, even if only for a few months.

Thanking God at all times, even in difficult situations, is important. Based on my life experiences, I am one to think on the positive side of things, and to think the best of people, especially believers in Christ Jesus. Paul began many of his letters by giving thanks to God for the churches he founded with God's help. Today we begin a series of sermons on the epistle of Paul to his beloved church in Philippi, a city in the northern part of what is now Greece. In this, as in other letters of Paul to congregations established during his apostolic mission, Paul writes of issues that he and they have to solve, but not before thinking about the positive and thanking God for that.

In this message, I look at the words of gratitude Paul offers for the Philippians to begin this letter. Maybe we will see some parallels between Paul's gratitude almost two thousand years ago and ours today. Always giving thanks for the great things God has done for us, including for us as a church, the Second Spanish Baptist Church of New York, for so many years, is good and right. Let us look at some aspects of gratitude in Paul's Epistle to the Philippians.

Aspects of Gratitude in Philippians

First, the context of gratitude is *prayer* (Philippians 1:3-4). Paul thanks God for the Philippians in his prayers; he continually prays for them. I think that today we should thank God for all those who have prayed for this congregation through the years. In the well-known church Christian Church John 3:16 in the Bronx, for many years there was an elderly woman named Sister Agosto (no relation to my family as far as I know) who was noted for her prayer. What's more, there was a time in the history of this church when she had a special place in a corner of the large pulpit of John 3:16 where she sang and praised the Lord during the devotional part of the service. When the time came for preaching, Sister Agosto would kneel down to pray for the preacher, especially when it was the great founder and pastor of the church for many years, the Reverend Ricardo Tañon. Thank God for sisters and brothers who pray. I'm sure that here at Second Baptist there are prayer warriors—sisters and brothers who stand out for their spirit of prayer.

3

Please pray for me, and I promise I will pray for you. The apostle Paul prayed for his churches.

Second, Paul gives thanks to God for the *fellowship* or *partnership* of this church (1:5,7). Paul thanks God for the faithfulness of the Philippians to share with Paul and his ministry. What is this partnership? The Greek word that Paul uses here is *koinonia*, which is sometimes translated as "communion" or "community" or "sharing." In English the word *partnership* gives the sense of an agreement between apostle and church to share in the Pauline mission. For example, we learn later in the letter that the Philippians have contributed financially to Paul and his apostolic mission (Philippians 4:10-20). However, more than a material gift, the Philippians have given to Paul spiritually, with their prayers and with the love they have exhibited to him, especially during this time that Paul has been in prison for the gospel (1:12-18). The Philippians sent one of their own, the local church leader Epaphroditus, to represent them in person before Paul. In fact, Epaphroditus even got sick fulfilling this service (2:25-30). In many ways, therefore, the Philippians have supported and shared with their apostle (1:7).

Brothers and sisters, mutual support is of utmost importance in ministry in order for the church to grow and succeed. Without the support, prayers, and participation of many in this church for so many years, both when you had a pastor and you didn't, there would not be a Second Spanish Baptist Church these many years after its founding. We need *koinonia*—mutual cooperation—with one another to move forward and plan for a secure future.

Third, Paul believes in the *hope and love* of the church in Philippi. Paul has no doubt in the future of this church, that what God began will remain until the last day (1:6). I like the historical perspective of verses 5 and 6: "from the first day until now," until the end when Christ returns for the church, God will continue to work on behalf of the church, "perfecting" it, making it better and better in love and good deeds. What's more, Paul calls the church to have love, using the Greek term *agapē*, which stands for having a genuine concern for someone other than ourselves. Paul also wants the church to practice careful "discernment," engaging decision-making processes that carefully study options before "approving" (Gr., *dokimazō*), what is best for the community moving forward. Thus the church needs to make good and insightful decisions now so that on "the day of Jesus Christ" the church will be "pure and blameless" before God (1:9-10).

Brothers and sisters, our hope is intertwined with what we do as a community of believers. Alone one cannot be a good Christian. Yes, salvation is an individual decision, but *living* salvation and reaching it in the end has to be done in community and with love and insight to make good decisions for the well-being of all. So we need to live out our faith *together* to ensure the ongoing well-being of the Second Spanish Baptist Church. Each one of you, in your own way and with your own gifts, has much to offer this church and community. We need one another to grow in love, faith, and hope. And we need leaders—pastoral, diaconal, administrative— to love and to love one another for "the defense and confirmation of the gospel" of Jesus Christ (1:7), whether in good times or bad. Second Spanish Baptist Church has endured because you have practiced faith, love, and hope. We all have to continue to follow that path.

Finally, Paul writes about the *compassion and justice* the church must practice. A church cannot be the church without compassion and justice (Philippians 1:8,11). Paul says that he "longs" to see the Philippians because of "the compassion of Christ" that drives him (1:8). What has secured the growth and well-being of Second Baptist has been, in large part, the compassion of your previous pastors, who have deeply and sincerely loved this flock. My personal experience in the pastorate, though brief, in Brooklyn, Boston, and Hartford, has taught me that one has to have a real pastoral call to make this work. In many ways, the spiritual hope of an entire community of people depends on pastoral ministry and lay leaders. And that is a big responsibility. Finding a good pastor is not easy. Nor is being a lay leader easy, because he or she must balance secular work and family time in order to serve the church of God. We need that *agape* love to "overflow more and more in knowledge [of how things *are*] and insight [deep wisdom of how to *do* things]" (1:9).

As part of love and compassion, Paul hopes that the church will produce a "harvest of righteousness" (Philippians 1:11). Righteousness or *justice* (Gk., *dikaiosunē*) involves not only individual "uprightness" or "personal morality," but also standing publicly for social justice. The church, to be an authentic church, has to be concerned not only for personal evangelism, but also for social justice in the name of that *evangel* who calls us to live and proclaim "good news," the good news of Jesus Christ. We have to do justice on behalf of our neighbors, especially those in need, and in that way share good news with them.

Years ago, after finishing my undergraduate studies at Columbia University, I got a job in the East Harlem College and Career Counseling Program, helping young high school students in East Harlem and nearby neighborhoods get into college. I did this job of academic counseling for two years (1977–79) before entering seminary in September 1979. Therefore, accepting your invitation to be your interim pastor is in some ways a return to this very historic and important neighborhood of the Latino/a community in New York. One of the questions I ask and that we should ask together in the coming months is "What 'fruits of justice' can we deliver to the community that surrounds us here in East Harlem— the historic 'barrio Latino'?" I know that many of you live nearby and some a little farther away, and still others even farther, but together we are called to be responsible for those around us, as Paul wants the church in Philippi to love and serve the people around them. We will see more of this in the sermons on Philippians to follow in this series. In any case, Second Baptist Church, the community of East Harlem and surrounding areas needs a church that cares for the spiritual, social, and economic well-being of its people. May God help us to show compassion and produce fruits of righteousness and justice.

In thanking God for the Philippian church, the apostle Paul wants the people of Philippi to know the compassion he has for them, the love that he expects them to practice with one another, and the fruits of justice he hopes they will produce on behalf of those who surround them.

Conclusion

On this day in which I start a few months as your interim pastor, Second Spanish Baptist Church of New York, just like the apostle Paul gave thanks for the church at Philippi, I thank God for your historic presence and ministry for so many years. Together we thank God for the *prayers* of the saints of this church over the years, because without them you would not have survived as a church given all of the problems that can destroy any church anywhere, especially these days.

We thank God for the *fellowship—koinonia*—and mutual support we feel for one another, without which the church cannot be church. We thank God for our leaders, who feel *compassion* for each of us and for the *love—agapē*—that each of you practices for your brothers and sisters both inside and outside the church and its surroundings. We need compassion for the needy in our community.

We thank God for the opportunity to produce *fruits of justice*, whether providing a glass of water to the thirsty, a plate of food to the hungry, a piece of clothing for the naked, or shelter for the homeless. Indeed, God calls us to denounce the systems that exist which allow there to be thirst, hunger, poverty, and homelessness.

This is part of being the prophetic church of the Lord Jesus Christ. We have to practice good judgment to *approve* (*dokimazō*) actions we must take as a church in order to produce righteousness and justice (Philippians 1:9-10).

And we thank God for our *hope*. Paul asserts that what God started in us, God will finish (1:6). Today I celebrate with you, the great Second Spanish Baptist Church of New York, that what God started here, God will bring to completion. Thanks be to God for this great hope!

Second Church, repeat after me these three Greek words, which can be a mark of our ministry at this stage of your life as a church: *koinonia*—partnership; *agapē*—love; *dokimazō*—careful discernment and approval. Do you dare learn a little Greek with me and, most of all, deliver some words of vision for our church? *Koinonia, agapē, dokimazō:* We want to be a united community, a community of love, and a community that uses good judgment to determine its future in light of its past. Amen? Amen!

> **Prayer:** *Dear God, thank you that we are a church that practices gratitude and love with faith—a gratitude that acknowledges your presence in this church for so many years and a love that strives for the well-being of our brothers and sisters and of those around us in need of help and blessing. Bless our church and help us be a source of peace in a world of pain. Now and forever, we pray. Amen.*

A Personal Note on This Sermon / In the sermon I make reference to the East Harlem College and Career Counseling Program, where I worked for two years after college before going to seminary. This was an important community agency that began in the 1970s and is still active in East Harlem. It helped young people from surrounding Latino/a and African American communities get information and assistance with applying to college. As a counselor in that program, I helped young people with their college selections and applications, and frequently we planned college trips to places such as Boston, Providence, and Ithaca so that students could see campuses, since many of their parents were not able to make such trips.

One of the unique things about the history of this agency, which I discovered later, was that one of the founders, Sue Alexander, used to work for the famous East Harlem Protestant Parish ministry. The latter began in the 1950s under the leadership of George (Bill) Webber, to help historic mainline Protestant churches in East Harlem connect better to the changing demographics and needs of East Harlem. Webber later became president of New York Theological Seminary, where he served from 1969 to 1983. So I was reconnecting to these historic New York religious roots, and the social service agenda of the gospel, which I reference in this sermon, by serving both New York Theological Seminary and the tradition of social action that George Webber brought to it in his presidency, and Second Spanish Baptist Church and its deep and historic roots in East Harlem.

A few weeks later, on Mission Sunday at Second Baptist, I preached a sermon on one of my favorite passages in all of Philippians, a section in which the apostle Paul praises leaders who helped him carry out his missionary ministry throughout the Eastern Mediterranean, his associate Timothy and local church leader Epaphroditus.

2
Leaders for
the Mission

Philippians 2:19-30
Sermon preached on April 28, 2013

I hope in the Lord Jesus to send Timothy to you soon, so that I may be cheered by news of you. I have no one like him who will be genuinely concerned for your welfare. All of them are seeking their own interests, not those of Jesus Christ. But Timothy's worth you know, how like a son with a father he has served with me in the work of the gospel. . . . Still, I think it necessary to send to you Epaphroditus—my brother and co-worker and fellow soldier, your messenger and minister to my need. . . . Honor such people.—Philippians 2:19-22,25,29

This Mission Sunday we want to emphasize the type of leadership needed to carry out the mission that God entrusts to us as God's church. Thus we continue our series on Paul's letter to the Philippians by looking at Philippians 2:19-30, where Paul praises leaders in his mission because of their service and sacrifice. And we also ask ourselves how can we be "salt and light" as in the passage from Matthew we read at the beginning of worship, which is the theme for this Sunday of missions throughout the American Baptist Churches in the United States (Matthew 5:13-16).

Timothy: Servant Together with Paul (Philippians 2:19-24)
First, let me point out some key aspects that help us understand the
leadership of Timothy:

■ Paul appreciates Timothy's commitment, including his enthusi-
asm, dedication, and concern for the well-being of the church and
the needy, following the example of Christ's sacrifice and service
(see Philippians 2:1-11).

■ Paul also emphasizes the service of Timothy, who stood with
Paul in the mission. Such was Timothy's service, learning from and
supporting Paul, that Paul considers him like a son: "Like a son
with a father he has served with me in the work of the gospel"
(2:22). To be able to serve in God's work alongside mentors that
can guide us toward deep and fruitful leadership in the mission of
God's church is a powerful idea.

Second Church, whatever happens with the question of pastoral
leadership, it is very important that the church is always looking
for, giving an opportunity for, developing and supporting the work
of local leaders who can serve the mission of Second Baptist for the
long term. What will happen when transferring from one generation of pastoral leadership to the next if we are not up to date in
considering who will be the next trustees, deacons, teachers, and
outreach ministry leaders? On whom do we have to rely to walk
together with the leaders of today to ensure who will be the leaders of tomorrow? Who our next generation of leaders will be is an
important question for this congregation and for any church that
seeks to serve God and community for the long haul.

Have you asked yourself if you are up for the challenge to be a
leader in God's kingdom? You have to walk close *now* to someone
who can mentor you in faith and service as Timothy did with Paul.
For example, the youth who are serving with our excellent audio-
visual leader upstairs are learning that ministry well today so that

they can exercise it or some other ministry in the future with continuity and excellence when current leaders are no longer with us.

Therefore, we take note of the key Greek word for "service" in this passage on Timothy: *diakonia*. Let us add this to the other Greek terms we have learned from Philippians—*koinonia, agapē,* and *dokimazō* (partnership, love, and proper examination or discernment). *Diakonia* indicates service beyond my own interests on behalf of the needs of others. In what ways can we be leaders of the mission of Second Baptist Church who can serve with a spirit of *diakonia?* This is part of the great challenge for us today.

On Friday night, for my birthday, Olga and I went with our children, Joel and Jasmin, to have dinner. Then we saw a tremendous movie, called *42,* about the great African American baseball player Jackie Robinson, who broke the color barrier in the major leagues in 1947. It's an inspiring movie, and I recommend it to all of you, whether you like baseball or not. (I do!) One of the things that drew my attention to the film was the courage of Jackie Robinson, the valor with which he gave of himself to this historic task. He simply wanted to have the opportunity to play baseball at the highest level. He had the talent. But in time he realized that the opportunity to break the racial barrier was long overdue, and so it was a responsibility and a service—a *diakonia*—to this nation, although the nation as a whole didn't want to go there.

About a decade after Robinson broke that color line, a minister of the gospel—a Baptist, by the way—the Reverend Dr. Martin Luther King Jr., led the nation beyond that moment. However, it was Jackie Robinson (himself reared a Methodist, as God uses Methodists too), using his talent in baseball and his spirit of *diakonia,* who opened the way so that Dr. King and others could lead the way to even more great heights in our identity as a nation and in fair and just practices as a people. Both Robinson and King, in their own way, brought the good news of justice and love to the heart of this nation.

What is your *diakonia* to the mission of the church? How can you be faithful to God's call on your life to help a world in need of love, service, and faith?

Epaphroditus: A Servant Who Took a Risk for the Mission
(Philippians 2:25-30)

Another aspect highlighted in the movie *42* was the great sacrifices that Jackie Robinson endured. Rejection, insults and verbal abuse, and even physical attacks came his way, for example, when racist pitchers threw at his head. Yet Robinson kept his dignity and control. He had a mission, a *diakonia*. In this passage from Philippians, we find a figure less known in New Testament history, but we learn of his importance in the Pauline mission: Epaphroditus. Let's look at what made Epaphroditus one of Paul's favorite leaders.

First, he was a brother, collaborator, and fellow soldier (Philippians 2:25), that is, an important "fellow worker" in the Pauline mission. Epaphroditus seems to be important in many practical ways. He is the one who brought an offering to Paul from the church at Philippi during Paul's imprisonment, as we learn in Philippians 4:10-20. In fact, Epaphroditus reminds me of a few key leaders in this church, those who do a little bit of everything—Bible study, finances, building care, as well as representing the church at external events and keeping an eye on the well-being of your interim pastor! So, you are contributors, fellow soldiers, faithful workers in the struggle of work for the Christian gospel and mission. Such was the leadership of Epaphroditus.

In addition, Epaphroditus also had an important role as a representative of the church at Philippi to the Pauline mission, in this case, during Paul's imprisonment. Epaphroditus was a Philippian church messenger—a "sent one"; in Greek, *apostolos*! So he was an apostle from the Philippians to Paul. At heart, the term *apostolos* is a missionary term. Epaphroditus travels to do his ministry with Paul on behalf of his home church, the Philippian congregation. And that ministry is *leitourgos* in the Greek (literally, "public working"), from which we derive our English word *liturgy*. Eventually, *leitourgos* in the Greek world came to refer to the work of pagan temple leaders in worship of the gods. So Epaphroditus's service in this case may be considered a form of "worship," a praise to God. By serving Paul on behalf of the Philippians, he praised God. This is the type of person and leader Epaphroditus was; he served in a number of capacities and he did so as a form of worship delivered to God and for the cause and mission of the gospel.

So what happened to Epaphroditus during this faithful missionary service? He got sick, Paul tells us, to the point of death: "He was indeed so ill that he nearly died" (Philippians 2:27). Paul is happy when Epaphroditus recovers and is finally able to return to Philippi. Paul asks that the Philippians receive and honor this faithful servant and collaborator, and all such leaders in the Pauline mission (2:29).

Sometimes in our service and leadership in the mission for Christ, we sacrifice time, money, and even (if we are not mindful of self-care) our health. We invest ourselves for the welfare of many. We often put so much of ourselves into church service, and sometimes very few notice. Nonetheless, persons who serve in the church mission in these ways deserve to be received as Paul asks for Epaphroditus: with joy, with great esteem, and with gratitude for such service and sacrifice. Indeed, we hope that others will enlist in the leadership and service to God and God's church as a result of our example. But do be mindful: we are not always going to be appreciated, recognized, or imitated. However, we need to move forward in response to the mission that God has entrusted to us. We need to keep chugging along, working at it for the good of all, for we are leaders called to the service, the *diakonia*, of God.

Conclusion

One of my favorite novels is called *Bel Canto* by Ann Patchett, which depicts a rebellion in a fictional country in South America. A group of revolutionaries, most of whom are young people, invade a party of the country's ruling elite and a hostage situation ensues. After a while, the young revolutionaries and the elites bond, and little by little the talents of young people, many of them with little education because of the nation's unjust poverty, especially among rural populations, come to the fore.

For example, the character Ishmael learns to play chess with some of the business professionals in the group. Ishmael learns quickly and becomes a brilliant chess player. A Japanese interpreter to Spanish for the foreign group of elites in their midst begins to teach the young rebel Carmen to read and write in English. She, too, learns her lessons so quickly that soon she is the interpreter to English for the veteran leader for this group of young people, who only seeks justice for his beleaguered community. And another young man, Cesar, begins to practice with an opera singer who was hired to entertain at the party. With a little training from her, he starts singing like a pro. Hence the book title, *Bel Canto*.

Surveying this scene toward the end of the novel, the rebel leader exclaims, "It makes you wonder. All the brilliant things we might have done with our lives if only we suspected we knew how." Oh, if we only knew how good we could truly be! By the way, the novel ends tragically, and I will not say much more, but I will never forget that scene of those young people, learning and demonstrating so much talent in so many ways, which they never realized they had.

In God's church, given the mission that lies before us, we have no time to waste. We need to find the hidden talents in our midst, provide opportunity and training, and send people out. Paul sent Timothy to the church in Philippi. The church at Philippi sent their local leader Epaphroditus to help Paul in his hour of need. Everyone in Paul's circle had a mission; their *diakonia* was clear, and Paul and the church entrusted it to them. Dear friends of La Segunda, God allows us to recognize our gifts and talents and to develop them with study and practice, and then he launches us to the mission of Christ. Now is the time! Amen!

Prayer: *Dear God, may we recognize always the need for good leadership in our midst, leaders whether pastoral or lay, who care for our church, our members, and the communities we serve. Keep calling leaders for the vineyard, dear God, because the work is great and the laborers are few. The apostle Paul, your servant, recognized the need for help in the mission you had granted him. Thank you for those diakonoi who walked by his side. Bring us more of the same in this day and age, we pray. Amen!*

A Personal Note on This Sermon / My greatest avocation is reading good literature, mostly fiction (when I am not reading books on the New Testament or catching up on current events). Ann Patchett is a favorite novelist, and *Bel Canto* is the first novel of hers that I read years ago. It has stayed with me, especially that storyline about the hidden talents of those impoverished Latin American young people. Fact met fiction in Patchett's description. Whenever I have an opportunity to include that story or others like it in a sermon about the need for leadership development, especially among the "least of these" in our Latino/a church communities, I do so with great joy, although sometimes church folks (who are used to hearing just the Bible story unpacked) are surprised by my choices. Nonetheless, I move forward in using snippets of good novels in my sermons with Latino/a churches and all others as well.

The final two sermons of the series on Philippians took me to two of the most well-known passages in this letter, one in which Paul reflects on the goals of his ministry and life, and the other in which he summarizes the great Christian virtues of excellence and good thinking.

3
Proceeding toward the Goal

Philippians 3:12-16
Sermon preached on May 5, 2013

Not that I have already obtained this or have already reached the goal; but I press on to make it my own, because Christ Jesus has made me his own. Beloved, I do not consider that I have made it my own; but this one thing I do: forgetting what lies behind and straining forward to what lies ahead, I press on toward the goal for the prize of the heavenly call of God in Christ Jesus.—Philippians 3:12-14

I don't know about you, but I'm not perfect. Just ask Olga, my dear wife, whom many of you have met and know what a straight shooter she is. She tells it like it is, and that includes my shortcomings. I thank God for her. In any case, the apostle Paul exhorts the congregants in Philippi to be "perfect." Let us see why he would say such a thing and what, if anything, such an exhortation has to do with us. Is "perfection" at all possible?

Leading Up to Our Text (Philippians 3:4-11)
Paul has just exhorted the Philippians, who are faced with opposition and difficulties, to keep their eyes fixed on Christ, ready to consider the past of their lives as "rubbish" in comparison with the

"surpassing value of knowing Christ" (Philippians 3:8). We must remember that this does not mean that we forget the past, or that we do not honor all the good of our past. But in comparison to our new life in Christ, argues Paul, the things of the past, especially those that turned us away from God, should be discarded. So we believers should put our past in its proper perspective, especially in light of our new lives in Christ. Remembering the past is important, as long as we know that we can move forward positively into a new future.

For example, in Paul's case, his life as a member of the Pharisaic party in the Judaism of his day had its limits. He followed the rituals and laws of his religious traditions, and he did so well, he writes in Philippians 3:4. Yet he had come to an understanding in his own life that approaching God in a ritualistic, formulaic way was not sufficient. In Christ, Paul found a personal relationship, true and lasting. Previously, although he was excellent at fulfilling his religion's expectations, he did not feel the satisfaction of fulfilling his relationship with God to the utmost. He found that doctrines and rituals without closeness to God in a personal way (which for him eventually meant relationship through Christ), left him short in fulfilling his complete humanity. The rules and rites of religion are not enough, Paul teaches here. Rather, a personal relationship with God through Christ counts the most. For those of us who claim the Christian faith as our own, this belief in a relational God made known through the person and work of Jesus Christ is foundational to our faith.

Perfection (Philippians 3:12)

Okay, but *perfection*? How is that possible? Surely even a personal relationship with God in Christ does not lead to perfection, does it? It depends on how one defines *perfection*. In Greek, the term often translated as "perfect," is *telios*, which literally means "perfectly whole or complete." Thus, for Paul, Christ believers are in the process of becoming "whole" or "complete." We strive for "perfection" in terms of "wholeness." Indeed, for Paul, the ultimate goal for the believer is to attain resurrection just as Jesus did (Philippians 3:11-12). This goal includes knowing Jesus better every day, trying to live as Jesus did, including facing difficulty and suffering, until reaching our final salvation in new life ("resurrection") after our physical death. There is perfection, that is, "completion," in such a search, as we reach that final goal, which begins with life in Christ in the present and also in the "beyond" for eternity.

Of course, continues Paul, that ultimate goal of eternal life has not been achieved in this life. Therefore, in that sense we are not "perfect"—complete in everything. Perfection for Paul is about completion, and we are not there yet. All this is in process, writes Paul: "Not that I have already obtained this or have already reached the goal; but I press on to make it my own, because Christ Jesus has made me his own" (3:12), that is, Christ began the process of final salvation and resurrection, and one day it will be achieved. But for now that goal is not met. The concept of perfection, *telios*, means both the goal and the fulfillment of the goal. So if the goal is resurrection, Paul still lacks that. Rather, we all are in process. I continue toward the goal. Final perfection eludes me, but I am headed, slowly but surely, in that direction because in Christ, God has called me to "be perfect," complete, whole, "saved."

I preached my first sermon more than forty years ago when I was eighteen years old. It was a Friday night in a youth service. Needless to say, I was not very good. I have preached many sermons since then, and by God's mercy, I have slowly but surely gotten better. Nonetheless, every time I stand in a pulpit it is a challenge because I know that although I prepare well, I am imperfect and God is not finished with me yet. As the old gospel hymn says in Spanish, "*La lucha sigue, o Cristiano!*" ("The struggle continues, dear Christian!").

Part of that struggle is to improve the skills and gifts that God has given us, to pursue the goals that God has for us, imperfect as we are, to be better preachers, teachers, administrators, brothers, sisters, fathers, mothers, sons, daughters—in short, better believers in the Christian faith. We each are a work in progress, no matter what our skill set, calling, expertise, or desire to do well. There is always a learning curve, new goals to determine and achieve. In short, nobody is perfect, but we can certainly shoot for the best, with God's help.

The Relationship between Past and Future
(Philippians 3:13-14)

If I am in the process of reaching the goal, what do I do *during* that process? What do I do *now* to get *there*? Of course, many answers can be offered for how we should behave as believers in Christ in the here and now, but Paul offers two answers in this context. First, he argues that we should not care too much for the past. Rather, we are to keep the past in proper perspective as we move forward toward the future.

Therefore, second, he exhorts the Philippians to extend themselves toward the future. The image Paul describes is of an athlete in a race who, when nearing the finish line, extends the chest to cross the finish line first. If a runner takes even a quick look back, he or she might fall, or someone might overtake him or her. The runner's gaze needs to be set on the finish line. Any deviation could mean the loss of the race. "Don't look back," Paul exhorts. The past already happened, including, as a runner and believer, your preparations; you did the necessary exercises to prepare for the race; you trained well. Now it's a matter of keeping your eyes set on the end goal.

In his first Olympics in 2008, Usain Bolt, the great Olympic track star, had already won his race but could have set a brand-new record. He had it in hand, but he looked back to his competition (no one was close) and then extended his hands out before the finish line in a too-early celebration. He lost a valuable few seconds. He had already won the race but began to pose for victory when he could have stayed the course just a few more seconds and set a new world or Olympic record. Friends, let us keep our eyes on the prize of heavenly citizenship, as Paul describes it in Philippians 3:20, no matter what distractions come our way. With the help of God we will arrive.

At those same 2008 Olympics, Michael Phelps, the champion swimmer, was in second place in his meet. He was going to miss the chance to pass the record of seven gold medals for one Olympics set by swimmer Mark Spitz in 1972. However, Phelps kept pushing himself and won the race by a fingertip! I remember Phelps's mother putting up two fingers at the end of the race to indicate that her son had finished second. But, "No, Mom!" He kept pushing and beat out his competition by a fingernail. Paul wants Christians to have an even more successful race to the finish. Therefore we must keep looking forward: *What is the next challenge? What else can I learn? Who else can I help?* Keep on pushing forward! Don't look back!

Our Church and Its Future

Being a church with eighty-five years of history is a good thing. Also good is reflecting on that history and how much has been achieved. Think about all the people over all those years who worked hard to establish, develop, and maintain this ministry. Nonetheless, the question for us today is "What now?" What future awaits us?

How can we reach our goals as a church, including the ultimate goal described in the great christological hymn earlier in Philippians: "At the name of Jesus every knee should bend, in heaven and on earth and under the earth, and every tongue should confess that Jesus Christ is Lord" (2:10-11)? As we proceed to assure

21

ourselves of that final goal, that fulfillment, that "perfection," what do we do as a church, as a people, as a community? In which direction does God want us to go? What goals do we set for ourselves? How do we achieve "perfection," that is, "completion"?

Another Way: "The Heavenly Call of God"

In Philippians 3:14, Paul writes, "I press on toward the goal," to the finish line. The goal is described as "the prize of the heavenly call of God in Christ Jesus." I am fascinated by that phrase, also translated, "the sovereign calling of God" (in Spanish, "*la soberana vocación de Dios*"). It speaks to the aim of God: to call all of humanity to eternal salvation, but to do so through our "vocations" in the world today. We all have a call from God that one day will end in eternal salvation, our "final vocation," fulfilled through Christ Jesus. But for the here and now our lives should be a "vocation," a calling dedicated to God in Christ Jesus, and all that Jesus stands for—love, justice, peace, and human well-being.

Therefore, we must set goals in the present to reach that ultimate goal. We must do so as individual believers but also as part of a community of faith. I am sure there are brothers and sisters here today, both youth and adults, who have goals for their lives: study, work, build a family, grow in faith. These are important goals, and we must continually work on them. There are youth here who have a sense of calling, whether to minister in the church or in their secular work, with faith. They ask themselves, "How can I use my job out there in the world as a response to God's call on my life?" The search for an "earthly" vocation can be carried out in the context of God's "heavenly vocation" for our lives.

Young person, you can use your studies and choose a secular career even for the glory of God. When our youth and adults have goals for their lives, clear goals with plans with which to achieve them, that is a wonderful thing. Even better is when they know that they can strive toward those goals in the context of life in Christ who calls us to make God's appeal here on earth. We can use our vocations, whatever they may be, for the glory of God and God's people. In all of this, we know that our vocation *par excellence* is to surrender our lives to God so that we can have a secure future: "the heavenly call of God in Christ Jesus." I pray we can submit our lives to serve God, including with our jobs, our vocations, our careers, for the greater glory of God, who calls us each day to do God's will.

Recently I read a newspaper article about a Hartford family that long ago had big plans to get rich; the father of the family was writing a play that he hoped would have great success and bring great wealth to the family. It didn't happen: a failed family goal. Yet the parents and the children reoriented their goals. No, they wouldn't make a lot of money or become big-time celebrities. But they reoriented their lives toward education and community service. Today the grown-up children of this family are well known in Hartford for their advocacy and community service but not for their wealth. Even failures in our lives can always be used with the help of God to begin new goals that ultimately serve humanity even better.

Coming to the End (Philippians 3:15-16)

In the final analysis, Paul believes that there is perfection—in the sense of maturity. Maturity is a form of perfection. Paul writes to the Philippians that all who are "mature" (*telios*—"perfect," "complete") should feel that our life *together* is an integral part of the sovereign calling of God: "Let those of us then who are mature be of the same mind" (3:15). Community unity is part of our maturity in Christ as the church, even if we are not all alike in history, looks, or talents.

Paul expects a congregation to travel together in its service to God. This is a kind of perfection as well, even though in verse 12, Paul indicated that we as individual believers, and certainly not the church as a whole, are not perfect because we are still on the way *toward* achieving our individual and collective goals. Yet, while complete perfection is not possible, a measure of maturity is. The Greek term *telios,* translated as perfection, means three things for Paul: "end or goal," "fulfillment or completion," and "maturity." Perfection in Paul means "end" or "goal," but also maturity—achieving a measure of maturity or completeness.

So, there are no perfect Christians. Nonetheless, if there are believers more mature than others in the faith, these can be role models for others. Paul makes this point explicit in Philippians 3:17: "Brothers and sisters, join in imitating me, and observe those who live according to the example [*typos*—'model'] you have in us." Those who are mature in faith should feel the sovereign calling of God in their lives to help others. Indeed, they may be helping others recognize a sense of God's call on their own lives.

Friends, every believer here can be an aid to the revelation of the sovereign calling of God in the lives of our brothers and sisters. However, if you are a mature person in the faith, do not use your maturity to disparage someone who still lacks a certain "perfection." Rather, let us all try to "be of the same mind" (Philippians 3:16), which is the original exhortation of this letter in 1:27-30, the unity in Christ that must sustain a community in good times and bad times. Therefore, we must go forward—unanimous in faith—Paul concludes in this beautiful passage of Philippians 3.

Brothers and sisters, we are a mature church, with many mature people in the faith. More than eighty-five years of ministry produce such a reality. But the work is not over. Mature believers have to make way for those who are new in the faith, who perhaps are yet to be "perfect," that is, more complete and confident. Yet, just as much, often, as the mature in faith, new believers nevertheless have much to offer. But we must open the way in the coming years so that we can see the development of new believers in the faith, mature and complete, full of the sovereign vocation of God in their lives through Christ Jesus.

Conclusion

Let us not, as the "mature ones," forget the exhortation of Philippians 2:5-11 on the humility of Christ, who is our model of excellence. The story is told of a young girl visiting the beach with her family one day. She sees thousands of starfish stranded on the beach, dying for lack of water. She begins to throw them back into the water, one by one. Of course, the task is daunting because there are so many starfish. A man comes up to her and chastises her for even trying. "How can you possibly make a difference?" he taunts. After thinking about it for a moment and almost walking away, the young girl comes back and begins to throw more starfish into the water, one by one, exclaiming with each toss, "It made a difference to that one!" and "It made a difference to that one!" Soon her family joins her in rescuing the starfish, and then other people on the beach join. Even the man who had tried to stop the little girl joined in the rescue effort. Soon all the starfish were safely back in the water.

The young girl had resisted the insistence of the grown-ups on the beach, the mature ones, who told her it was not worth trying to rescue the starfish because there were so many of them. The young girl insisted instead that she could rescue each one, one by one, and that would make a difference for every individual starfish. Her hopefulness and maturity shone through, even for one so young. "Let the little children come to me," Jesus said, "for it is to such as these that the kingdom of God belongs" (Mark 10:14). We do not think we are so mature that we cannot learn from one another about this Christian walk, a walk so difficult sometimes that we do indeed need mutual help. We all have goals for our lives. Let us help each other achieve them for the glory of God.

My dear brothers and sisters, how can you change the world, little by little, with your partners here in this church? How can your spiritual maturity be used to make changes for the next generation, to help set goals and accomplish the mission of this church?

Together you can reach the target with the sovereign vocation that God has given you in Christ Jesus, including the call of God for this particular church in this particular corner of the world. And let us never underestimate those young people, who can teach us the way as much as anybody else. Together we are stronger, maturer, and more perfect than is ever possible alone. May God bless us to achieve our goals, now and forevermore. Amen!

> **Prayer:** *In our imperfections, dear God, you call us to a sovereign vocation of service with goals and expectations each step of the way. Help us to learn from each other—young and old—how to carry out our calling with a sense of wanting to be whole—mature and complete—even as we strive for that eternal salvation that will be ours only at the end. In the name of the Christ who calls us into this journey of learning and growing, we pray. Amen!*

A Personal Note on This Sermon / I first read the story of the little girl on the beach in an important book, recently reissued, by psychology professor and dean of Mount Holyoke College, who later became president of Spelman College, Beverly Daniel Tatum: *Why Are All the Black Kids Sitting Together in the Cafeteria? And Other Conversations about Race* (1994; 2017). In the book, Dr. Tatum addresses the issue of difficult race relations in this country, including among our young in schools. She ends the book, however, with this sense of hopefulness exhibited by the young girl on the beach saving the starfish, that if we start in small ways, with dialogue and conversation across difference, difficult as it may be, change will come. The story has remained with me for many years, such that I retell it whenever I want to encourage congregations to embrace change, even by starting out in small but meaningful ways.

4
Peace and Excellence in Service and Life

Philippians 4:4-9
Sermon preached on May 19, 2013

Rejoice in the Lord always; again I will say, Rejoice. Let your gentleness be known to everyone. The Lord is near. Do not worry about anything, but in everything by prayer and supplication with thanksgiving let your requests be made known to God. And the peace of God, which surpasses all understanding, will guard your hearts and your minds in Christ Jesus.

Finally, beloved, whatever is true, whatever is honorable, whatever is just, whatever is pure, whatever is pleasing, whatever is commendable, if there is any excellence and if there is anything worthy of praise, think about these things. Keep on doing the things that you have learned and received and heard and seen in me, and the God of peace will be with you.—Philippians 4:4-9

Ending well is important in life's endeavors, whatever they might be. Once when I was preaching in Puerto Rico on the theme of excellence, an outstanding youth orchestra followed my sermon. They were so good, so elegant and exquisite in their music making, a wonderful example of excellence in music ministry, especially for a group so young. That experience ended well. The orchestra exemplified what I had just been preaching about—caring so much about your faith and your service that you do all you can to be excellent.

Paul ends his passionate exhortations in his letter to the Philippians with a series of summary exhortations, and although they appear as generalities, they actually exemplify the excellence for which he hopes his congregation will strive. Whatever we start, we ought to finish well. Paul ends his letter to the church at Philippi with encouraging words, familiar to us in our Christian traditions.

Joy and Peace (Philippians 4:4-7)

First, the theme of joy and rejoicing, especially amid difficulty, that has echoed throughout the letter is repeated here. But even at the end, we still ask, "How can one be joyful in the midst of sickness and difficulty?" For Paul, the joy of which he speaks is not a question of feeling but of fact. As the old gospel chorus teaches us, "I have a joy in my soul, joy in my soul, joy in my soul and in my *being*." It has little to do with how I feel at the moment, but with the sense of security that God is real in my life, that no matter what, I am safe and secure in God.

In another context, Paul exclaims, "Where, O death, is your victory? Where, O death, is your sting?" (1 Corinthians 15:55). If even death has its proper place in our worldview such that we not ultimately fear it, our faith should transcend more transitory events and feelings that sometimes keep us down, sad, oppressed, anxious, and worried. Our faith keeps us focused on the ultimate reality of God's transcendence and on the ultimate victory in God exemplified by Christ, who overcame death on a cruel cross with the victory of resurrection and an empty tomb.

Joy transcends the immediacy of the immediate and is a deep, profound sense of happiness and security in God's presence no matter what our situation, a presence that consoles us and strengthens us for the long haul. We find contentment in the long-term, permanent presence of the divine in us, despite the short-term worry when things do not quite go the way we envisioned or expected. God is still an on-time God, a God of peace, a God of hope. We must carry with us, in good times and bad, a long-term vision. What does God have for us—today, tomorrow, and beyond? There's joy in that sense of anticipation and assurance.

Not only are we joyful people, but as a result of our security in God, we are people who live life with "gentleness"—gentleness, kindness, grace—a disposition of generosity and service but one that comes from the heart, not out of obligation. Giving testimony of kindness attracts people because we make "bonds between people," which is at the root of this word "kindness." Even knowing that "the Lord is near," Paul asserts, encourages us to work for people with a spirit of kindness that guides us.

The next exhortation has to do with "eagerness" and "worry." "Do not worry about anything," Paul writes, meaning, I think, that instead of worrying to the point of despair and debilitating anxiety, we pray. Yes, let us pray. God answers on God's time. God is an "on-time God"; in due time God responds. Of course, as a saying that Olga hangs visibly in our home reads, "God answers prayer and sometimes the answer is 'no'!" This hurts because we want God to say yes all the time. But sometimes, for mysterious reasons, the "no" of God is necessary in ways that stand beyond human understanding.

However, there is still peace (v. 7): "the peace [tranquility, security, well-being, *shalom, irenē*] of God, which surpasses all understanding." Although we sometimes do not understand it, this peace of God is transcendent, beyond our immediate comprehension, yet it keeps us and protects our hearts. For Paul, "heart," is everything that we are—soul, body, and spirit—and everything that we think, and God protects that because we are sons and daughters rescued by the work of Jesus Christ. I do not understand all the mysteries of how God acts in our lives, but I have "the peace of God, which surpasses all [human] understanding." We firmly believe that God is in control; we trust in God, which gives us inner peace although everything around us, even physical illness, is out of control.

Our Magnum Opus

Recently, while TV channel surfing in a moment of relaxation at home, I found one of my favorite films, *Mr. Holland's Opus*. This movie is about a musician who takes a position as a music teacher in a high school while composing a piece of music that he thinks is going to make him famous one day. But the years go by and he continues to work in the school, while his "magnum opus" languishes. Seemingly, there is no fame for this man, only the interactions he has with his students from year to year. In the film, some of his students become soldiers, administrators, musicians, political leaders, and even a state governor.

By the end of the movie, after some thirty years, Mr. Holland's teaching career comes to an abrupt end because of budget cuts in the school system. He gathers his things from the music room where he presided for so many years. However, as he leaves with his family, he hears a commotion in the school auditorium. When he enters, teachers, students, friends, and family have gathered for a celebration in his honor. Even the governor of the state, one of his first students, whom he had inspired not to break down in the midst of difficulty, joins in the celebration. She introduces many of Mr. Holland's students over the years, who are there to join the school orchestra, which will finally play his precious composition, and, of course, Mr. Holland will conduct the orchestra himself!

If you haven't seen this movie, you should, for it beautifully depicts the story of this music teacher, who has felt all along that his life had been a failure because he didn't get to do what he thought he would do, but at the very end he realizes the impact his teaching had on his students all those years.

This beautiful film makes me cry each time I see it. Here is a man who did not have peace in his life because he thought he had failed. However, he did have a tremendous impact on the lives of his students; they were his quintessential musical work, "Mr. Holland's Opus." If the character of Mr. Holland were portrayed through a faith perspective, he might realize that despite feeling out of control of his life for thirty years, God was in control and using his life for the well-being of others. Let us have peace and joy, no matter what happens. Let us believe that God uses us to bear witness to all the good in this world. Just like Mr. Holland learned to appreciate his contributions to a larger cause than his personal fame and success, God will use us to do good and to bring peace and joy to the lives of others. For this we need to trust God and rest on God in peace and faith. Let us allow God to use our lives for good, even the seemingly small things in our relationships with others.

Thinking the Best: Excellence in Faith and Ministry
(Philippians 4:8-9)

One more exhortation culminates this passage. Peace and joy include thinking the best. In verses 8 and 9, Paul emphasizes the importance of good thinking in our faith and practice. He begins with a list of positive values on which we must think: truth and honesty, justice and purity, kindness and care for a good reputation. This is not to say that we do not love what is hard to love, particularly people difficult to love, or people of bad reputation out there. We must love such people and seek ways that integrate them into the community of faith to improve their lives. But there are issues and activities that we are wise to avoid because they lack love and ultimately fail to produce good testimony, which I believe the apostle has in mind here. In the end, activities, customs, books, television, movies, friendships—anything that has "virtue," writes Paul, is worthy of our attention and Christian practice. "Virtue" in this text is the Greek word *aretē*, also translated "excellence." All of these are values that lead to praise, and it is, in fact, their excellence that merits such praise and sense of worthiness. Focus on these, exhorts Paul. "Think about them!"

A good thought life is critical for a peaceful, happy daily Christian life. Such a thought life takes effort, careful planning, and good choices. Sometimes we make mistakes about what is pure and just, and what makes for a good reputation and what does not. One person's judgment about what is good and pleasant and worthy of excellence is another person's downfall. Some people should not eat or drink certain things because such things might do them harm; others, however, can handle those same things in moderation. We need to select carefully what we see or read or hear. Think carefully about what is worthy of your attention, focus, and life choices. God will help you.

This morning I read a report on the health of immigrants to the United States.[1] The first generation of immigrants, we learn from this report, tends to live a few years longer than their sons and daughters eventually do, because the latter adopt North American diets and habits and therefore develop health challenges that our ancestors never had. Can you believe that? My generation may live shorter lives than my parents' generation because of our health choices! We must "think about these things" and make better choices. I myself confess to weight issues. I must make better food choices and exercise more. This is part of what it means, I believe, to be thinking Christians, those who seek and practice excellence—*aretē*—in all we do and say!

In such endeavors, we receive help from good examples (Philippians 4:9). If we learn good things from good models of faith, let's put those things into practice. Years ago, when I was just age fifteen, a young preacher came to my church in Brooklyn. He had completed his bachelor's degree and a master's in Bible and theology—and he had a background similar to mine. He was a Puerto Rican Pentecostal, like me, just a few years older. In short, he struck me as a good role model for me to follow. Years later, when I was in college, I saw him again. He was completing his doctorate and serving as a professor at a seminary in Boston. A few years after finishing college, I went to study with him and three years later finished my master's degree in theology. Then he needed an assistant for a theological education program he was running in Boston for inner-city pastors, so I went to join him yet again. I ended up working with him for twelve years while I finished my own doctoral program in New Testament studies.

That role model and mentor, and dear friend, Professor Eldin Villafañe, still teaches in Boston. He encouraged me to sow my own oats in the teaching ministry, so I moved on to Hartford and now New York all these years later. Yet he became one of those from whom I "learned and received and heard and [saw]" (Philippians. 4:9). Many of the things I do now in teaching and ministry, and indeed in faith, I "keep on doing" because he taught me first.

Who are your exemplars and mentors today? From whom can you learn to live lives worthy of God and Christ? From whom can you learn to be faithful and fulfill the will of God in your life?

Conclusion

Finally, these exhortations of Paul—to rejoice in all things, and to think and practice excellence—end up ensuring peace. "And the God of peace will be with you," Paul concludes in verse 9. The God of peace will be with you. At the end of his career, Mr. Holland realized that his life was worthy and that he should have peace. Many people arrive at the end of their lives and do not have peace because they wonder what was it worth. I so loved hearing the testimony of our sister Viterba Ortiz during the Friday evening service, when she recounted her years of life and service. At ninety-seven years old, she testified that if her time comes in the next few years, she is at peace that she did what she could for the Lord's work, especially with her seventy years as an active member and leader of this church.

Brothers and sisters, "if God is for us, who is against us?" (Romans 8:31). Who can be against us if we belong to the God of the universe? Put your trust in Christ who will make your joy complete. In Christ we find the joy of life and peace. But we must work to think about everything that is good, everything that is right, everything that brings good testimony, everything that is excellent—that has virtue—*aretē*. It is not easy; but with God's help we will do it! Brothers and sisters, we will do it. We are and will be servants of Christ Jesus who practice excellence in service and life!

> **Prayer:** *May the peace and joy of Christ reign in this place, in our families, and in the community that surrounds us, now and always. And may we always be, dear God, with your help, people of faith who do our best in all that we endeavor, learning well from good exemplars that you put in our paths. Amen!*

A Personal Note on This Sermon: Summary of Sermons on Philippians / At the end of this sermon on Philippians 4:4-9, our last in the series on Philippians as a model of Paul's congregational ministry, I encouraged the church to continue on our journey toward excellence, by remembering the list of values we learned from this letter of Paul to the Philippians, using some of the Greek terms to jog our memories:

- *Koinonia:* community
- *Agapē:* love
- *Dokimazō:* discernment by testing and approving
- *Diakonia:* service

- *Telios:* goal, fulfillment, perfection
- *Aretē:* excellence

I also used the Philippians discourse to help us make a confession of faith: *Let us be, with the help of God, a united community that practices love for one another, carefully discerning the will of God for us as individuals and as a church in service to humanity with clear and fixed goals, exercised with excellence.*

Then I encouraged the church to think about developing a mission statement for themselves that strove for something like this, again based on the sermons from Philippians:

> Our mission is to be an authentic fellowship that practices God's love and discerns carefully what is God's will for our lives, both as individuals and as the church, so that we might serve each other and the neediest in our communities. We strive to have clear goals and know that God by the Holy Spirit gives us the means to complete them, and to do so with excellence!

Note

1. Sabrina Tavernise, "The Health Toll of Immigration," *New York Times*, May 18, 2013.

Part Two

The Vision for Church and Leadership in the Book of Acts

In the summer of 2013, I preached a series on the Book of Acts, beginning with a Pentecost Sunday celebration of the "miracle of communication" (Acts 2:1-13). A second sermon focused on leadership for the Latino/a church, reminding the congregation that leadership may come "in all sizes and shapes" given what we learn from Acts 6:1-7 and its aftermath. The apostles asked for deacons to "wait on tables" so that the apostles could concentrate on preaching the Word. Yet in Acts 7 and 8, we get some of those deacons preaching the Word themselves (Stephen and Philip). After several sermons on the ministry of the apostle Paul in Acts, I concluded the series with Paul's farewell speech to the Ephesians (Acts 20), exploring the qualities of Paul's exemplary ministry that we can learn from today, especially when we need new leadership for a new day.

In the first sermon in this section, I asked Second Spanish Baptist Church, a congregation in transition, to consider what new modes of communication are needed for the twenty-first century Latino/a church in the city. I wondered with the congregation what we shall do about the growing language issues in many Latino/a congregations. La Segunda is historically Spanish-speaking, but as our communities change internally and externally, with more and more Latino/a young people in the church speaking English than Spanish, and more and more of the church's neighbors being English-dominant or speaking other languages—what is the church to do to fulfill its mission in that neighborhood?

5
Communicating God's Wonders

Acts 2:1-13
Sermon preached on May 26, 2013

When the day of Pentecost had come, they were all together in one place. And suddenly from heaven there came a sound like the rush of a violent wind, and it filled the entire house where they were sitting. Divided tongues, as of fire, appeared among them, and a tongue rested on each of them. All of them were filled with the Holy Spirit and began to speak in other languages, as the Spirit gave them ability.—Acts 2:1-4

Last week was the day of Pentecost on the ecclesiastical calendar, but we will reflect on it today, beginning with a series of sermons on the Book of Acts and the vision of the church we see in it. *Pentecost* means "fifty days" and referred to the fifty days of harvest in the calendar of ancient Jewish holidays. In early Christianity, it came to refer to the fifty days after the death and resurrection of Jesus Christ, when the church received the Holy Spirit (Acts 2:1-13) and welcomed its first new believers (2:37-47). This latter passage we read by the end of Acts 2, after the sermon by Peter that explained to the Jewish pilgrims gathered near the Jerusalem temple what the experience of receiving the Holy Spirit meant (2:14-36).

In my sermon this morning, I want to focus on the meaning of this experience from two thousand years ago for us today. In the final analysis, Pentecost has to do with the miracle of communication and not so much with the miracle of tongues, as many interpret today. Indeed, we must ask ourselves today, how do we communicate the wonders of God to "all the nations"?

First, a Reading of Acts 2:1-4

Sometimes, Acts 2 is read as a miracle of heavenly, angelic languages, such as what the apostle Paul wrote about in 1 Corinthians 13:1: "If I speak in the tongues of mortals and of angels, but do not have love, I am a noisy gong or a clanging cymbal." But here in the book of Acts, although speaking these "tongues" may be the result of a powerful spiritual experience, they are not like a noisy gong or a clanging cymbal. These tongues convey the truths of God for all to understand! They are not angelic tongues of a superspiritual experience, which usually bless only the individual speaking, as Paul argues in 1 Corinthians 14. Rather, we are told that languages were distributed on that first day of Pentecost so that the recipients of the Spirit could communicate to those gathered at the temple from foreign nations, as we read in Acts 2:3-4. In that way, all who were near could understand a new empowering message from God in ways that communicated to them.

The author of Acts, the evangelist Luke, demonstrates this purpose in Acts 2:5-11. First, "devout Jews from every nation under heaven" were present on that first day of Pentecost. They heard their own languages being spoken (v. 6). Not only that, but also those speaking their languages were "Galileans," among the poorest Jews of all Israel in those days. The pilgrims to Jerusalem that day wondered, *How is this possible?* God was certainly involved!

To emphasize the miraculous and diverse nature of this event, Luke provides a list of nations present, from just about everywhere in the ancient Mediterranean world: "Parthians, Medes, Elamites, and residents of Mesopotamia, Judea and Cappadocia, Pontus and Asia, Phrygia and Pamphylia, Egypt and the parts of

Libya belonging to Cyrene, and visitors from Rome, both Jews and proselytes, Cretans and Arabs" (Acts 2:9-11). Most were Diaspora Jews from these regions; some were Gentile converts to Judaism ("proselytes"). They were all together at the temple of Jerusalem to celebrate the Jewish feast of Pentecost. Yet something other than crops were harvested that day in Luke's telling of the story!

Why would I read out all these strange names (some familiar) in your presence today? The point is that the people from the whole world, strange places and all, were present to hear the message of the wonders of God in their own languages. This was made possible by the Holy Spirit, and this is the way the church of Jesus began, by communicating the wonders of God in intelligible ways. Recall the apostle Paul's words in 1 Corinthians 14:18-19: "I thank God that I speak in tongues more than all of you; nevertheless, in church I would rather speak five words with my mind, in order to instruct others also, than ten thousand words in a tongue." On the first day of Pentecost, languages known to thousands of people from all over the world were spoken by pilgrims from small, obscure, nearby Galilee.

Pentecost for the Present Day

This passage has left me thinking this week about our reality here in our church. For almost eighty-five years, Second Baptist Church has been a Spanish-speaking church, and will continue to be for years to come. There are still many who need to hear the message of the wonders of God in the language of Cervantes (the sixteenth-century writer who practically invented our modern Spanish language), Santiago (your long-time beloved pastor, who oversaw the construction of this beautiful worship space in 1963 and who lead you for thirty years until 1985), and Orlande Costas (the great evangelist and Baptist professor of the 1970s and 1980s who was an inspiration for me, a young preacher and doctoral student, before his tragic death from cancer in 1987).

Yet today in 2013 other languages are spoken in this church and around us. Some of us speak both Spanish and English with equal ability, and some of us speak one better than the other. There will be some, perhaps a lot of our sons and daughters, who, although they understand Spanish, prefer to hear about their faith and the gospel of Jesus Christ in the language of Shakespeare, Billy Graham, and Martin Luther King Jr. However, they still want to be Latinos and Latinas and not Anglo American or African American. They want to be "devout" Latino/as (Acts 2:5) who let the Holy Spirit use them to communicate the wonders of God in the ways most available to them. In addition, there are many others, especially outside our walls here, who speak only English. Many are coming up from 96th Street to 102nd Street, 104th Street, and 116th Street, from Park Avenue to Lexington to the East River. And they want a genuine experience of the wonders of God! Many will say, "Well, there are churches for them too." However, what if God put us here eighty-five years ago to minister to everyone around us? And what if God wants us to speak different languages—Spanish, English, Spanglish, and even French if Haitians come to our doors as well! I am not saying what we *should* do, but I am asking, what if God wants us to be open to the possibilities of the Holy Spirit coming down and distributing tongues in this place for a new Pentecost?

Peter's Message in Acts 2:14-40

In response to the coming of the Spirit in Acts 2, Peter preaches, "These are not drunk, as you suppose." Rather, the prophet Joel predicted that "your sons and your daughters shall prophesy," "your young men shall see visions," and "your old men shall dream dreams" (2:17). These are all groups—daughters, sons, elders, children, youth—who are present in our church. As a result of all generations participating, said Joel and Peter, "Everyone who calls on the name of the Lord [invoking Jesus as our identity and authority] shall be saved" (2:21). When Peter finished, there were many conversions (2:41), and the church—diverse in age and culture—persevered in good teaching, strong sense of community, and constant prayer (2:42).

There is nothing wrong with considering the change the Holy Spirit can bring to our lives as individuals and as a church as in Acts 2:1-4. Are we ready for the "rumble"—"the rush of wind"—that God can bring to the Second Baptist Church in the years ahead? I think we can be. So be it! Amen!

> **Prayer:** *Dear God, thank you for the gift of language. Thank you for calling our ancestors in the faith to use their languages, with the help of the Holy Spirit, to reach the diverse peoples of their world. We celebrate the Spanish language that has been at the heart of La Segunda's ministry for so many years, reaching out to the Spanish-speaking communities throughout East Harlem and beyond. Help us to discern in the coming years how the Spirit will lead us to continue to be a church that celebrates the gospel of Jesus Christ, in response to the needs of our increasingly diverse surroundings, in language and languages that recognize who our neighbors are and how we can best present the gospel to them. In the name of the One who is your Word among us. Amen!*

A Personal Note on This Sermon: Language in the Twenty-First-Century Latinx Church / One of the challenges facing the Latinx church has to do with the issue of language. As historically Spanish language–dominant churches become fewer and the children and grandchildren of Spanish-speaking people become English dominant and lose some or all of their Spanish, how should we conduct our worship and teaching? Different churches have different answers. Some create parallel or separate services in English. Some conduct bilingual services, where everything or parts of the service are done in both languages, a very difficult task, usually not done well in my experience. (Imagine being a thoroughly bilingual person and having to hear the same thing twice in a service!) Others decide to hold the line and see themselves as preservers of the Spanish language, even in an increasingly English-dominant Latinx culture. Still others, who were founded as majority Puerto Rican churches, for example, have decided to maintain their Spanish-language worship and Sunday school because newer generations of immigrants to their communities need to worship in Spanish. Whatever decisions are made, this sermon proposes that the Pentecost model projects that we convey the gospel message in culturally and linguistically productive ways.

6
The Life of the Church

Acts 2:42-47
Sermon preached on June 2, 2013

They devoted themselves to the apostles' teaching and fellowship, to the breaking of bread and the prayers. Awe came upon everyone, because many wonders and signs were being done by the apostles. All who believed were together and had all things in common; they would sell their possessions and goods and distribute the proceeds to all, as any had need. Day by day, as they spent much time together in the temple, they broke bread at home and ate their food with glad and generous hearts, praising God and having the goodwill of all the people. And day by day the Lord added to their number those who were being saved.—Acts 2:42-47

"I believe in the growth of the church!" So said the late, great Latino theologian and my dear friend, Dr. Orlando Costas, upon seeing my first-born son, just several months old, for the first time in 1986. "I believe in the growth of the church." He said it joyfully to celebrate with us becoming parents for the first time, but as a student of the church's mission, he was serious in his love for the church and the possibilities for its growth. New children helped just as much as new converts! I, too, believe in the church—its importance, its potential, and its service in the community in favor of those in need of spiritual, moral, and physical strength.

What are some basic elements of what it is to be church according to the memories of the early church? A reminder from time to time, like those given to us by the Book of Acts, is of utmost importance, especially for a church in transition.

A Committed Leadership (Acts 2:42-43)

The teachings of the first apostles (v. 42) and their actions (v. 43) were worthy of respect ("fear" in terms of "awe") in this community. Participants in this incipient church community witnessed the commitment of their leaders, a commitment to change and transformation demonstrated by "miracles and wonders." The church still needs leaders who teach well and who demonstrate what it is to have faith in God and wait patiently for the work of God. Our church today has had good leaders for many years. That's what has ensured its growth and spiritual development for so long. The question before us is, how can we continue to develop good leaders and how can we ensure that they grow in their faith, gifts, and talents for greater service to the church?

Perhaps your interim minister can help in that regard. Indeed, we must work together in the time we have to ensure that such identification, growth, development, and preparation of the next generation of leaders for our church continues to emerge. I believe in the importance of good leaders, including "apostles," that is, missionaries and outreach agents for the church. We must ensure that a new generation of church leaders is *always* on the way. Are *you* a future leader of the church, one who does God's will and teaches God's truths? Or maybe you simply want to learn more so you can be a teacher and practitioner of God's truth? Listen to the voice of God calling you into leadership for the church!

A Church United and Committed to One Another
(Acts 2:44-45)

Church should be a place where we share what we have so that no one is lacking. We should seek a system of internal finances, against unjust systems outside the church, like the primitive church did, so that no one is left hungry in our community, including those who may not be official members of our church. We are still responsible, as the church of Jesus Christ, for those in need in our surrounding neighborhoods. This is especially true in places like East Harlem. Obviously, some have more than others in terms of material things. It was easier for the early church to sell properties and share the results. Today this is not so simple. Nonetheless, we need to continue to look for creative ways so that those in a position to produce wealth, goods, and services can share them with the "least of these" as Jesus taught us (see Matthew 25:31-45).

We have a tax system in this nation that is supposed to be established so that those who have more can help those who have less. We know that not every government program works well in that regard. We need the church to be vigilant so that their parishioners and neighbors receive help when it is needed most. What are ways that people who know how to create wealth can share their good fortune with those in need, including in and through the church? The church that is generous in its giving and sharing, both internally and externally with those outside the community, will always be a church that is highly regarded and "evangelistic"—sharing the good news of the *evangelio*!

Unity and Praise within the Temple and Beyond
(Acts 2:46-47)

Part of being the church is to *attend* church. We have a nice temple, all paid for, to celebrate our services and meetings. But in this day and age, we need activities and programming that draw people to the temple. It can't be "business as usual." People need to feel that in praising, singing, praying, preaching, and teaching their needs are being met. But there is so much more that we need to do. Like the early believers, people need to feel that they are welcome to sit at the table and share bread, be it Holy Communion, a regular meal of fellowship, or simply a productive conversation with a brother or sister in Christ. Usually "breaking bread" together opens the door for such dialogue, learning from one another about who are we, what we care about, what the needs are in the community, and how we can help meet those needs.

Such interaction is important not only in the temple but also in our homes and neighborhoods, with those who are immediately outside our faith community. If we reach out with love and concern, we will have opportunity for people to consider us with favor and gratitude. And in that way, we will share the gospel of good news about Jesus Christ and his faithful love. It is also important to practice the skills of being a church within our homes, including in our marriages and the mutual leadership that is needed with wives and husbands. We should also prepare our sons and daughters to one day assume leadership in their homes, jobs, and the church. Toward that end, we should ensure that the physical and material needs of our spouses, and of our sons and daughters in terms of their education, are nurtured. The church, Acts tells us here, is a reflection of our home and our homes of our church.

Conclusion

At the conclusion of this passage, Luke calls us to have favor with those outside the church and we shall thereby see the church grow. Growth takes place because we are involved in community issues and because the community, realizing the interest we as a church have in their well-being (even if they make no commitment to the church), will perhaps begin to show interest in what we are offering as a church and will join us in this adventure of faith.

In one of my favorite movies, the baseball film *Field of Dreams*, the protagonist, played by Kevin Costner, heard a voice telling him, "Build it and they will come." So he built a baseball field in his cornfield, and long-gone baseball players showed up to play the game they loved once again. However, by the end of the movie (spoiler alert), what is brought to light was that Kevin Costner's character had an unresolved relationship with his father. The baseball field helped heal that long-lost relationship. The church should be a center of restoration, a place for individuals and families to unite, and for the community seeking a connection with the divine and with fellow partners in life's journey to find a long-lost home.

Our Metro New York Association for the American Baptist Churches has a summer project this year for children. It is a way for the church to reintroduce themselves to the community. We will look forward to ways to implement the program here in our neighborhood. With committed leaders, a united church, and a spirit of service in word and deed, much can be achieved, as our earliest forebears in the faith demonstrated. Indeed, we continue to "believe in the growth of the Lord's church" as taught to us by that great pastor, Baptist teacher, and theologian of mission, Orlando Costas. Amen!

> **Prayer:** *Dear God, may we as a church grow by caring: caring for each other, caring for those who surround us with such great need, and caring to see the good news of Jesus shared with all. Help us to be a growing church by giving of our talents, time, and treasure to build a beloved community both inside this community of faith known as Second Baptist Church, and outside in our beloved East Harlem and beyond. These petitions we put before you, dear God, in faith, hope, and love. Amen!*

A Personal Note on Orlando Costas: Reminisces from All-Too-Few Encounters / Orlando Costas, referenced in this sermon, was a Puerto Rican evangelist, missionary, and theologian who taught in Costa Rica, at Eastern Baptist Seminary (now Palmer School of Theology), and at Andover Newton Theological School, which he served as dean from 1984 to 1987, the year he passed away all too soon from stomach cancer. He had been a prolific author in the field of missiology and also was a well-liked Baptist preacher and teacher who taught many young Latinos and Latinas who went on to become successful pastors, missionaries, and professors in their own right. I knew him when he came to Boston in 1984 to become dean at Andover Newton while I was working nearby at Gordon-Conwell Seminary's Center for Urban Ministerial Education.

When I first met Orlando, I was thinking about doing further graduate work after completing my master of divinity degree at Gordon-Conwell Theological Seminary. Although he barely knew me, Orlando invited me to his office early in his tenure at Andover Newton and sat me down to look at my academic transcript to see what graduate program might suit me best. I told him I wanted to study New Testament, and he said, "You might do better with theology or urban ministry, or better yet, urban missiology." He really wanted me to study with him, but later that year I was accepted in a PhD program in New Testament studies at Boston University, and he was happy for me.

A couple of years later, one of Orlando's prize students, Rev. Felix Carrion, who had been the student speaker at Andover Newton's graduation just a few months before, was being installed as a United Church of Christ pastor in Lawrence, Massachusetts. Orlando was the guest preacher. This was late 1986, and it was the first public outing of our son Joel, who had been born in October of that year. Olga and I were excited to introduce Joel to church life, and the occasion happened to be this ordination and installation of Felix, who had also been a friend of ours for many years.

After the service, Orlando came over to us, checked out our months-old boy in his baby carriage, and in a jovial, loud preacher's voice, as was his style, exclaimed, "*Yo creo en el crecimiento de la iglesia!*"—"I believe in the growth of the church!" It was his missiological way of congratulating us for adding a child to the world, and especially to the church world.

Roughly a year later, Orlando was on his deathbed from a ravaging stomach cancer. His beloved wife, Rose Costas, and the family had organized a round-the-clock vigil at his side in the hospital in Newton, Massachusetts. Several students, friends, family members, and colleagues would take turns spending the night with him so that Rose could get some rest. My night was spent watching this great man of God and letters sleeping, mostly uncomfortably, waking up to talk and then doze off again, get some water, move from bed to chair, and hear me haltingly read from Scripture. He loved the psalm I picked out for him, even though now, some thirty years later, I can't remember which it was. He also wanted to talk theology.

By then I was well into the second year of my doctoral work. He asked me—right there in that hospital room in the middle of the night—what I was working on. I told him I was researching the apostle Paul and his role as an urban mission leader. He apologized, unnecessarily as far as I was concerned, for not being as clear as he would like but that he remembered hearing about one of the books key to my study, Wayne Meeks's *First Urban Christians*, a book about Paul's social world. He was glad I was making progress. Then he dozed off into a deep sleep until it was time for me to go at daybreak. It was one of the most profoundly impactful nights I have ever spent in my life—watching a man die with dignity, faith, and still a sharp mind at work. I never saw him alive again, but those memories of him encouraging my search for a doctoral program, rejoicing at my son's birth, and affirming my scholarship even on his deathbed will live with me forever.

Orlando Costas had often been a guest preacher at Second Baptist Church in East Harlem decades before I got there. He had recruited several young people who came out of that church to study theology with him. I was honored to preach from the pulpit he had visited on occasion years before and to invoke his name in this sermon.

7

The Church and Its Leaders

Acts 6:1-7
Sermon preached on June 9, 2013

Now during those days, when the disciples were increasing in number, the Hellenists complained against the Hebrews because their widows were being neglected in the daily distribution of food. And the twelve called together the whole community of the disciples and said, "It is not right that we should neglect the word of God in order to wait on tables. Therefore, friends, select from among yourselves seven men of good standing, full of the Spirit and of wisdom, whom we may appoint to this task, while we, for our part, will devote ourselves to prayer and to serving the word." What they said pleased the whole community, and they chose Stephen, a man full of faith and the Holy Spirit, together with Philip, Prochorus, Nicanor, Timon, Parmenas, and Nicolaus, a proselyte of Antioch. They had these men stand before the apostles, who prayed and laid their hands on them. The word of God continued to spread; the number of the disciples increased greatly in Jerusalem, and a great many of the priests became obedient to the faith.—Acts 6:1-7

A church cannot function well without everyone doing his or her part. However, sometimes it takes time to determine who can do what, and what different gifts exist in the community of faith. I love the passage in Ephesians 4:11-12, in which the author writes that God gave gifts so "that some would be apostles, some prophets, some evangelists, some pastors and teachers, to equip the saints for the work of ministry, for building up the body of Christ." All believers—"the saints"—are prepared to carry out "the work of the ministry" so that the body of Christ may be built. God sends "apostles," that is, missionaries, and "evangelists," people who clarify well the gospel of Jesus Christ such that nonbelievers would be attracted to it, and "pastors and teachers," who instruct and guide the community. But notice how it is *all* the members of the church who operate the various functions that make the church grow and that build the body of Christ—inside and outside church walls.

Everyone counts in the church—the teachers who teach the children, the deacons who keep an eye on our spiritual development, the preachers who clarify God's Word, the trustees who watch over finance and property, the prayer warriors who think about each and every one of us each and every day so that we may be healed and blessed. Everyone counts! Leaders show us the way to make our gifts count. And this is for the well-being of all in the church and our community.

Problems in the Early Church

Our passage today from Acts 6 describes a problem of leadership and growth. It was a good kind of problem—more people had joined the community and therefore there was more complexity. What happens when people who do not speak the language are added? Who will help us? When the church grows, we need more and more help to keep it going and growing. Most early Christians were Aramaic-speaking Palestinian Jews, who are called "the Hebrews" here in Acts. But soon Jews from the outskirts of Palestine, including those who spoke Greek, converted to the gospel of Jesus Christ.

Unfortunately, in the practice of sharing the church's assets with the neediest in the community, widows—specifically those who spoke Greek and were not Aramaic-speaking widows from Palestine—were being excluded from receiving the aid they desperately needed. As Acts 6:1 describes it, they "were being neglected in the daily distribution of food." Greek-speaking widows were excluded from the help they needed simply because they did not speak the right language.

What could be done? Let's be clear, brothers and sisters, nobody wants to leave anyone out in the service of the church. However, sometimes there is so much need that we forget—to mention someone in prayer, to visit the shut-in or the sick. However, if we do not help one another, if we do not make that extra call, if we do not remind our leaders or the people who can and like to make one or more visits, it just does not get done! There is no evil intention. Nobody intentionally leaves anybody out in the blessings of the church; oftentimes we just need more people to care!

I do not think there was any evil intention among the early believers in not providing for the Greek-speaking Jewish widows as much as the Aramaic-speaking widows were receiving. There simply were not enough people helping out in those initial days of the formation of Christ's church.

A Proposed Solution

What could be done? Spreading the good news needed to be a shared task. In this case, after a meeting of all the believers (that is, of disciples in general), the apostles, being concerned that they were not able to preach the word freely if they had to worry about feeding the widows, proposed that a separate group of leaders would be appointed to ensure the fair distribution of goods to the needy widows. In this way the apostles could continue to preach the word, and a group of highly spiritual and wise individuals would "wait on (*diakounein*) tables" (v. 2). These leaders would focus on the material needs of the people. This was the beginning of what came to be known as "deacons" (and eventually in early church history, "deaconesses," to distinguish female from male deacons).

What were the *qualities* of these "table servers," the original meaning of "deacons"? They would bear good witness, that is, have a good reputation as people with good standing in the community. They would be "full of the Holy Spirit," being connected to God through God's daily presence. And they would be wise; that is, they would have a practical intelligence in how to get things done (v. 3). Good reputation, full of God's presence in their lives, and wise—practical intelligence in how to get things done! We need all of this and more in church life and in life in general in our own day and age!

It was assumed in these initial days of the Christian church that this "diaconal" ministry would be different from the ministry of the apostles, who were to persist "in prayer and in the ministry of the word." The apostles—founders of the church and its first traveling missionaries—would concentrate on preaching the word and offering prayers for the sick. Theirs was the public ministry of the word and public face of this newfound movement in Christ (v. 4). This public ministry was also a *diakonia* for the church—a service. Yet it was meant to be exclusively a ministry focused on preaching and healing, while the newly appointed "deacons" (*diakonoi*) would focus on the material needs of the community, especially the neediest among them in this ancient context, such as women without husbands or family to attend them.

It is true that in the church we need a public, out-front ministry. Sometimes—most of the time, actually—we also need behind-the-scenes people who do the most important day-to-day, nitty-gritty work of the church. We need everyone for God's work in this world!

What was the young church's reaction to this request by its leaders? Quite positive it seems. Acts 6:5 indicates that they held some elections and seven people were chosen. In this case, all were men and all of them had Greek names. This does not mean that these "deacons" did not include Jews at this early juncture in the church's history. But they were more likely than not multicultural people, perhaps Jews from the Diaspora, who could understand the Greek language in order to address the needs of the Greek-speaking widows (v. 5). These seven so-called deacons were multi-talented, multicultural, and multilingual. They were the ones needed for the job.

However, there was something more about these individuals besides their names, language skills, and culture. For example, the text describes Stephen as "a man full of faith and the Holy Spirit" (v. 5). In fact, they *all* were people of faith and the Spirit, and we shall see in the next few chapters of Acts that this is going to be very important.

Results

What were the immediate results of the selection of these servant leaders? First, the apostles laid hands on these seven individuals in prayer to authorize and bless them for the ministry they were about to undertake in service to the needy of the community (v. 6). Second, as a direct result of this arrangement and the appointing of these servant leaders, the church grew (v. 7). Even a number of Jewish leaders from Jerusalem, called "priests" here, joined the Christ movement, which was unified in its faith in and obedience to Jesus as the Messiah, the Christ.

Yet perhaps the greatest thing of all happens after our passage. As Luke points out in Acts 6:6, Stephen was a man filled with the Holy Spirit and faith. Eventually, besides serving the tables, sharing the goods, and helping with the widows, Stephen is used by God to proclaim the gospel! Stephen's service (his *diakonia*) goes beyond the immediate needs of those widows in the church. We learn from Acts 6 and 7 that Stephen gives a long speech before the council of Jewish leaders about how God has been working among this new movement of Christ believers, fulfilling God's ancient promises in the person and ministry of Jesus and now his disciples. As a result of Stephen's stirring sermon, opponents of the movement stone Stephen to death. His preaching leads to his stoning—the first Christian martyrdom recorded in the New Testament.

What happened? Was not the proclamation of the word to be limited only to the apostles? Why is this "mere deacon" also preaching and even dying for what he preached? Stephen had the talent, the calling, and the persistence, even unto death, to proclaim the good news of Jesus Christ. But, it started "at the tables." God used that experience to build toward a bold preaching ministry by Stephen. God used Stephen beyond what he was initially called to do.

Then there is the story of Philip, another of the seven "deacons." After Stephen's martyrdom, Luke tells us that an intense period of persecution ensued against the church in Jerusalem (Acts 8:1). Believers scattered away from the church's beginnings in that city (8:4). Sometimes God has to shake us a little to get us out of our routine. Philip begins to preach in Samaria, and has good results (8:5-8). Then the Spirit drives Philip south of Jerusalem to Gaza in the desert. There he meets a eunuch traveling from Ethiopia, "a court official of the Candace, queen of the Ethiopians, in charge of her entire treasury" (8:27). Philip preaches to him, and the African leader joins the movement for faith in Jesus as the Christ, now not just a Jewish Messiah, but a Messiah for all (v. 35). So, like Stephen, Philip also goes beyond his initial calling to help with the widows and begins to preach good news on the road. As a result, an African servant of the queen of Ethiopia converts to Christ.

What happened? Was not Philip a mere servant of the tables, such that preaching was limited to the apostles? Apparently not! Luke, the author of the Book of Acts, wanted to teach us that God uses us all to carry out his work—some serving tables, others in more public ministries, and still others in many variations of the ministry, all proclaiming the message of good news in word and deed. Some people get the message of love in Christ proclaimed to them when someone serves them a meal in their hour of need. Others hear it when a chance encounter along the road of life puts one of Christ's spokespersons in their path. God will use a variety of ministries from all of us to bring the good news of Jesus Christ to those in need.

Conclusion

The stories of the seven deacons, especially Stephen and Philip, remind me of the words of Jesus in Matthew 25:31-40:

> When the Son of Man comes in his glory, and all the angels with him, then he will sit on the throne of his glory. All the nations will be gathered before him, and he will separate people one from another as a shepherd separates the sheep from the goats, and he will put the sheep at his right hand and the goats at the left. Then the king will say to those at his right hand, "Come, you that are blessed by my Father, inherit the kingdom prepared for you from the foundation of the world; for I was hungry and you gave me food, I was thirsty and you gave me something to drink, I was a stranger and you welcomed me, I was naked and you gave me clothing, I was sick and you took care of me, I was in prison and you visited me." Then the righteous will answer him, "Lord, when was it that we saw you hungry and gave you food, or thirsty and gave you something to drink? And when was it that we saw you a stranger and welcomed you, or naked and gave you clothing? And when was it that we saw you sick or in prison and visited you?" And the king will answer them, "Truly I tell you,

just as you did it to one of the least of these who are members of my family, you did it to me."

God sends us to serve those in need either with our preaching or
just with our actions. When we do reach out to those who need a
word of faith and action, we are serving Christ each and every
time. Francis of Assisi is credited with saying, "Preach the gospel
always; when necessary use words."

Whether you serve someone in need with a glass of water or
word of salvation, in the final analysis, you are serving Jesus Christ.
Be it as teachers of the church, as members of the diaconal body,
the trustee board, the treasury, the choir, the worship team, men
and women's groups, youth, Kid's Club, or Bread and Life
Committee—whatever your function, your service, your desire to
serve here in Second Church, God can use you in a great and powerful and important way.

> **Prayer:** *Dear God, help every person in this church to use
> their talents, gifts, and leadership abilities every day to
> help at least one person. In that way, my sisters and
> brothers will soon realize that many will experience the
> blessings of God in their lives. This is my prayer for this
> church and for the universal church and its leaders every-
> where. Amen!*

A Personal Note on This Sermon / One of the resources from prior
reading and study that helped me write this sermon was an essay
that Justo Gonzalez, noted church historian, wrote many years ago
on Acts 6, which he titled "Reading from My Bicultural Place: Acts
6:1-7."[1] Gonzalez pointed out how Luke is merely introducing the
"deacon" story in Acts 6 to perturb the reader with what follows
immediately in two subsequent chapters. So-called deacons transcend the roles expected for them, roles supposedly limited to the

apostles as the community preachers of the Word. According to Gonzalez, in the Acts narrative the Holy Spirit is always subverting expectations and roles so that the newly established Christ community can keep on its toes and always be on the move. This was my plea, with Gonzalez's help, to the church that Sunday morning.

Note
1. Published in *Reading from This Place: Social Location and Biblical Interpretation in the United States*, Fernando F. Segovia and Mary Ann Tolbert, eds. (Minneapolis: Fortress Press, 1995), 139–147.

8
Peter and Cornelius:
Men in Transition

Acts 10:1-33
Sermon preached on Father's Day,
June 16, 2013

In Caesarea there was a man named Cornelius, a centurion of the Italian Cohort, as it was called. He was a devout man who feared God with all his household; he gave alms generously to the people and prayed constantly to God. One afternoon at about three o'clock he had a vision in which he clearly saw an angel of God coming in and saying to him, "Cornelius." He stared at him in terror and said, "What is it, Lord?" He answered, "Your prayers and your alms have ascended as a memorial before God. Now send men to Joppa for a certain Simon who is called Peter; he is lodging with Simon, a tanner, whose house is by the seaside." When the angel who spoke to him had left, he called two of his slaves and a devout soldier from the ranks of those who served him, and after telling them everything, he sent them to Joppa.—Acts 10:1-8

Thanks to these four fathers from our church for this reading from the Book of Acts about the characters of the apostle Peter and a Roman centurion named Cornelius, their visions, and their encounter.

This long passage is followed by another one, in which the Jewish apostle of Christ, Peter, addresses those gathered in the Gentile home of Cornelius (Acts 10:34-43), including these highlights:

■ Peter's personal acknowledgment that God does not discriminate: "I truly understand that God shows no partiality, but in every nation anyone who fears him and does what is right is acceptable to him" (vv. 34-35). All are welcome to participate in what God is doing for humankind through Christ Jesus and our acts of love and justice. Doing acts of justice brings us closer to God, to the heart of what God seeks for humanity.

■ Peter explains that he and his colleagues have followed in the footsteps of Jesus, proclaiming the gospel of peace through Jesus Christ (v. 36).

■ Peter and his colleagues were simply describing all the good that Jesus had done in healing the oppressed and sharing the good news of God's presence: "God anointed Jesus of Nazareth with the Holy Spirit and with power; how he went about doing good and healing all who were oppressed by the devil, for God was with him" (v. 38).

■ What was the result of the good that Jesus did, according to Peter? Crucifixion. "They put him to death by hanging him on a tree" (v. 39). But also, thanks be to God, resurrection (10:40)! Peter points out the irony of ironies in the Christian story: do the good, even if you die trying, but in resurrection we find hope. Even though Jesus was executed for doing good, he lived again, and his followers bore witness to his ongoing presence in the Spirit through their teaching, preaching, and just actions.

■ So here is the testimony of his disciples: "Everyone who believes in him receives forgiveness of sins through his name" (v. 43). This was the basic message that Peter and the first disciples shared in their world: Belief, trust in Christ, leads to forgiveness of sin and connection to the divine Creator.

As a result of this message, Cornelius, his household, and his friends join the community of faith in Jesus as the Christ. First, "the Holy Spirit fell upon all who heard the word. The circumcised believers who had come with Peter were astounded that the gift of the Holy Spirit had been poured out even on the Gentiles" (10:44-45). And then "[Peter] ordered them to be baptized in the name of Jesus Christ" so that they might become part of the community of faith in Christ (10:48).

Until that moment, only fellow Jews had joined Peter and the apostles in this new movement. This was such an important turning point for the church, as Luke tells the story in his Acts narrative! Peter recognizes this moment of transition in the life of the church: "Can anyone withhold the water for baptizing these people who have received the Holy Spirit just as we have?" (10:47).

God revealed to the first leaders of the church that they should give as many people as possible—whether Jew or Gentile, male or female, rich or poor—the opportunity to be part of God's plan for Christ's church. God was not about to discriminate about who could be part of God's community in Christ. Non-Jews? Why not? God's Spirit was falling on them, and so the baptismal "water"—as a sign of admission into God's family—was for them as well.

Who are we excluding from the family of God today? Are we not seeing, just as Peter did not see before he had his vision of unclean, forbidden foods (Acts 10:9-16), that God wants to bring a transition to our understanding of what the gospel is and for whom it is? This is a challenge for the church always. What are the new horizons that God has for us today?

Peter and Cornelius: Men in Transition

These passages in Acts 10 also make me wonder this Father's Day about the characteristics of the two major figures of the text—Peter and Cornelius. First, Cornelius was "a centurion of the Italian Cohort" (v. 1), so not only was he not a Jew, but he was also a

Roman soldier, a member of the imperial military that had conquered and continued to oppress the people of Israel. Yet, at the same time, Cornelius "was a devout man who feared God with all his household" (v. 2). He had even given of his own financial resources to help the poor in the Jewish territories, "and prayed constantly to God" (v. 2). Thus Luke presents him as an honorable man who treated people with justice and fair play, including those he was occupying as part of a military force. He was pious and spiritual, praying to the God of Israel and offering charity to those who were under his authority. As soldiers who served him testified, Cornelius was "an upright and God-fearing man, who is well spoken of by the whole Jewish nation" (v. 22).

While Cornelius knew about the God of Israel, he was not satisfied. God gave Cornelius a vision about how he could get to know God better: by sending envoys to Peter and his fellow disciples so that Cornelius might get a better understanding. When Peter finally reaches Cornelius, the apostle introduces the centurion to knowing God by knowing Christ Jesus. It was a matter of knowing in a personal way the God to whom Cornelius had been praying and in whose name he gave to the poor. Peter teaches Cornelius about how Jesus is the way to know that God more fully.

Also notice how Cornelius does not keep the information to himself but invites others to join him in his home to hear the good news that Peter has for them. Many share in the spiritual pursuits of Cornelius—his family, his coworkers, and his friends. I think this is a good model for all of us today, including fathers and mothers. Good news about Jesus is not meant to stay with us, or within the church only; it is to be shared with others.

Moreover, notice that Cornelius has a good start with his established practices of prayer and doing good. This is affirmed in his vision: "Cornelius, your prayer has been heard and your alms have been remembered before God" (10:31). When we practice good and just deeds in our lives, even if we are not sure what's next for us, we are headed in the right direction. God will show us the way. When we don't know which way to turn, sometimes it is best just to keep doing good for those who are immediately in our reach and need our help and attention. As we practice the good and pray to God for guidance, future steps and long-term plans will be revealed in due time. Cornelius needed to hear from Peter about the love of God in Christ, but it was his doing good and staying close to God in the meantime that made it possible for him to hear God's plan for his life eventually.

And what about Peter? Peter had a vision about Cornelius, who was having a vision about Peter. Both were men of prayer. In Peter's case, it was a matter of food and tradition that stood in the way of a new direction for his life. Would Peter be willing to change his ideas concerning whom he could associate with in order to do God's will? Can you "eat" the change God is making for all humankind? Can Peter be a man of transition, as Cornelius is willing to be, and both move in a different direction than the one to which they are accustomed?

Peter and Cornelius are two men who find themselves led by God in opposite directions from where their normal lives were going, and yet they are heading toward each other, with God beckoning them on. Three times Peter has a vision about eating what for him was "junk food." But it is only when he receives the visit of the Gentiles sent by Cornelius that he begins to understand that God is doing something new—not only in the life of Cornelius, but also in the life of Peter!

God has to teach us all that lesson: "What God has made clean, you must not call profane" (10:15). Let us be careful about what we reject and what we are accepting in our lives, and also about *whom*! God wants to open a new path, and sometimes the direction leads us where we least expect it.

Upon obeying God and visiting the home of the Roman centurion Cornelius, Peter realizes how big a change God wants to make in his life. Peter proclaims, "You yourselves know that it is unlawful for a Jew to associate with or to visit a Gentile; but God has shown me that I should not call anyone profane or unclean" (10:28). Peter understands that God is making a transition in his life and asks the key question in the passage to Cornelius: "Now may I ask why you sent for me?" (10:29). The rest is gospel history, as Cornelius answers: "So now all of us are here in the presence of God to listen to all that the Lord has commanded you to say" (10:33). In other words, "Talk to us, Peter; teach us what we should believe." Cornelius was ready for his moment of transition and transformation.

So, there you have it: two men in transition, heading in different directions than their lives were supposed to go and yet headed toward each other in God's plans.

Conclusion: Are We Ready for Change?

What transitions does God have in mind for our lives? Fathers and mothers, what is God asking from you and your families—any new plans in transition? Men and fathers, where does God want to take you with your roles—roles as men in church and society? Families, men and women, young people, kids, elders, how is God working in your lives?

Let us remember the words from Acts 2:17-19:

> In the last days it will be, God declares,
> that I will pour out my Spirit upon all flesh,
> and your sons and your daughters shall prophesy,
> and your young men shall see visions,
> and your old men shall dream dreams.
> Even upon my slaves, both men and women,
> in those days I will pour out my Spirit;
> and they shall prophesy.
> And I will show portents in the heaven above

> and signs on the earth below,
> blood, and fire, and smoky mist.

Are we ready for the transitions God has planned for our lives? Can we let our lives impact those in need who surround us? This is the challenge of today's passage from Acts 10, as I see it. How can God change our lives and our vision for the gospel—the good news about Jesus—in this world? Peter was minding his own business, praying, and getting ready to eat some good Jewish food, but God had other plans. "Try this!"

What change does God want us to test in our lives? What new doors does God want to open for us? Men, husbands and fathers, on this Father's Day, are you ready to take another look at your service to God, marriage, and family? Where is God leading, and will you show the way for others, like Peter did for Cornelius?

Church, we are in the midst of transition. It has already started. We not only eat Puerto Rican rice and beans but Dominican mangu and Mexican tamales. What other changes to our palates are on the way? Are you ready for what God has in store for us?

May God help us to be people who listen to the voice of God and respond to the call of transition, as men and women of this church, as fathers and mothers, sons and daughters, elders and young people. Change is coming—watch and listen, and pray. Amen!

> **Prayer:** *Dear God, prepare us for the change that is happening right now in our lives, in our families, in our church. Help us to be ready to hear your voice when you call us to engage transition and transformation. Strengthen us for the long haul of faith, where change is inevitable, but under your guidance it can be for good. Thank you. In the name of the Christ who calls us to heed your voice and embrace transformation in our lives. Amen!*

A Personal Note on This Sermon: Embracing Change / This was not the only opportunity to remind Second Spanish Baptist Church of New York of their transitional moment as I served them as interim minister, but it was one of the major moments on a Father's Day in which my series in Acts took us to the transitions of Peter and Cornelius, and how God changed them through the presence of the Spirit in a fresh way. I was urging the church here and throughout my tenure to embrace change, for their future would depend on it. This was also a transitional sermon in my Acts series, as we finished earlier passages with the original apostles and turned to two sermons toward the end of the book in which the apostle Paul was the main protagonist.

9

The Spirit and the Church

Acts 19:1-7
Sermon preached on July 14, 2013

While Apollos was in Corinth, Paul passed through the interior regions and came to Ephesus, where he found some disciples. He said to them, "Did you receive the Holy Spirit when you became believers?" They replied, "No, we have not even heard that there is a Holy Spirit." Then he said, "Into what then were you baptized?" They answered, "Into John's baptism." Paul said, "John baptized with the baptism of repentance, telling the people to believe in the one who was to come after him, that is, in Jesus." On hearing this, they were baptized in the name of the Lord Jesus. When Paul had laid his hands on them, the Holy Spirit came upon them, and they spoke in tongues and prophesied—altogether there were about twelve of them.—Acts 19:1-7

Since the day of Pentecost at the end of May, we have been studying the Book of Acts and the several themes that we find in it. For one, we have looked at the formation of the early church in Spirit and power in Acts 2, with the power of communication among the nations. We will come back to that topic in a minute. Second, we studied about the early church and the identification and formation of its leaders when we learned about the deacons of Acts 6 (and 7

68

and 8). Third, on Father's Day, we talked about the reaction of two men—Peter and Cornelius—to their new encounters with God and God's will for their lives and the lives of their families in Acts 10. What's more, in a recent Friday night Bible study, we saw a fourth theme illustrated in Acts 9, showing how God changed the life of Saul of Tarsus, how he was evangelized, and how we are to evangelize in ways that bring real change to people's lives. We should add time, prayer, and teaching to the task of evangelism so that it is also concerned with the discipleship of the new convert, as those around Paul were.

Finally, in a sermon last week [not included in this volume] we explored how the almighty and all-sovereign God directs the steps of the church with the presence of the Spirit, the formation of leaders, and the transformational encounters of men and women in the work of the church. Today I want to pause a bit to talk more about the work of the Holy Spirit in the church, using this passage in Acts 19:1-7 as a starting point.

When Being a Disciple Is Not Enough

Paul visits Ephesus, this great ancient city in what is now Turkey. He enters into dialogue with the disciples there—fellow followers, students in the faith, but apparently incomplete in their understanding of what it means to be a follower of Jesus. What was missing from their knowledge or experience? The text of Acts 19 tells us that they had not received the Holy Spirit when they first believed. They didn't even know what that meant (Acts 19:2). Now, we must be clear here, because Paul proceeds to teach not about the Holy Spirit per se but about Christ! And this is fascinating! The response to the lack of reception of the Holy Spirit is a baptism in the name of Christ (vv. 3-4). Paul asks them how their baptism, a symbol of entry into the community of faith, took place, and they respond (and I paraphrase), "We were baptized with the baptism of John."

Paul proceeds to explain that John's baptism was for repentance, that is, in preparation for the coming Messiah that John preached. Repentance—to "about face" from the desire to sin—is the first step, but not the only one or the last. Therefore, they had the baptism of John, that is, repentance, the desire to change their lives, but they still needed the presence of Christ in their lives through a baptism—a complete surrender—to Christ with the presence of the Holy Spirit, who makes God genuinely present in our lives in a daily and powerful way.

What was the reaction of these individuals to this new teaching that Paul gave them? They "were baptized in the name of the Lord Jesus," that is, they entered again into baptismal waters and received a new entrance into the family of God under the authority of the Jesus that John preached, but the Jesus who was now the Christ of the church and the Lord of the universe (19:5).

And what were the signs of this new baptism? First, there was the imposition of hands as a symbol of the transmission of the presence of God. Second, there was the reception of a new presence of God through the Holy Spirit, that is, God with us, separating us out for a new work in God's name. Third, there were new languages, such as when the church began on the day of Pentecost. That was when this same Spirit came on Christ's disciples for the first time so that they could speak in a variety of languages and communicate with people from all over the world in Jerusalem that day. These incomplete disciples of John the Baptist needed a fresh experience of God's presence in their lives, in the name or under the authority of Christ, to be able to communicate clearly and powerfully the great truths of God that hitherto were incomplete in them. Believers should not communicate wrong things; the Spirit of Christ helps us communicate with skill so that the message is clear, precise, and accurate.

Therefore, in fourth place, these disciples of John and now of Christ, were made ready—after being made new in Christ, after being baptized in his name, and after receiving the power of the

Spirit—to communicate in new and clear ways the good news about Jesus Christ. They are ready to prophesy (19:6), that is, to proclaim the good news of Jesus Christ in a way that clarifies the will of God for the hearers of their words.

Now, not only were the "disciples of John" something good, but they were more complete. There were twelve of them, just like the first twelve disciples of Jesus, and they became part of the community of Jesus's disciples. They had joined the first twelve, the first 120, and so on. How so? Now they understood more fully who Jesus was, the Jesus about whom John had prophesied. Now they were baptized under his name, becoming an official part of the family of God. Now they had the presence of God in their lives—the Holy Spirit of God, who would enable them to communicate well the great truths of God.

What Do These First-Century Disciples Have to Do with Us Today?

You have your ideas, but let me share some of mine. To be a good disciple of Jesus, we must continue to learn to see what new thing God has for us. It is good to be faithful and to follow Christ no matter what happens, but every day we hope to learn something new from God about our faith and practice, whether inside the church or outside.

I also want to receive every day a fresh experience of the Holy Spirit of God when I wake up in the morning, just in case I meet someone who needs a word of encouragement, edification, consolation, admonition, instruction, or the like. For example, yesterday, while some of you were doing street evangelism as part of a planned church program, I was teaching in the seminary. I arrived exhausted at 4:30 p.m. to the apartment above the church and took a nap because I had gone to bed so late the night before preparing for my class. In the midst of my nap, I received a call on the church phone from a woman who had received information about the church during the evangelism outreach. She needed prayer right then and a visit soon. At that moment, although I was half asleep, the Holy Spirit gave me a word, and I was able to minister to that sister by telephone, and soon some of you will follow up with a visit.

We have to be ready, and the Holy Spirit provides us that opportunity day after day. The Spirit of God is in the church and with us outside the church each and every day, using us sometimes in ways we least expect. Glory to God for that!

Finally, this passage reminded me that I want to belong to a family of God that is very active in God's work. In Acts 19 disciples, both male and female, were baptized and then emerged with the power of God to communicate God's truths to all people of every race and gender, youth and adults, children and elderly. Would you like to belong to such a community? Let us pray that Jesus Christ will always have the Second Baptist Church in a spirit of learning, a genuine baptism of God, and a real presence of the Holy Spirit so that we might communicate the great truths of God to a world that has so many needs. Amen!

> **Prayer:** *Dear God, always have us on alert when your Spirit wants to move us, to take new action, especially to share the good news of Jesus Christ for those who have yet to hear. Prepare us for the surprises that you might bring into our lives. Let your Spirit put us in the right place at the right time so that those ready to respond to your message of love and joy might have a ready ear by their side, one who listens, prays, and helps bring healing to a needy soul. Amen!*

A Personal Note on This Sermon / During my interim tenure at Second Spanish Baptist Church of New York, an American Baptist Churches USA congregation, I had the opportunity to perform one baptism. This one congregant spent time with me in preparatory classes for baptism; he was part of a longtime family in the church who was reintegrating himself into faith community, and he had never experienced adult baptism, which he very much wanted to do. It was an exciting moment for the congregation, this man's family, and him.

It might have been the Sunday I preached this sermon; I can't remember. However, I do remember the pomp and circumstance surrounding the event, and how the church deacons guided me through the process. (I had done only one other baptism in my career as a seminary professor and as a sometime interim minister twenty years before.) I thoroughly enjoyed welcoming this individual into the family of God after a brief interview in which he confessed his faith publicly before going under the water. Nobody felt any "fireworks" like those experienced by the people baptized by Paul in the Acts 19 passage. But the man and his family, and the entire church (including me) were overjoyed at the experience of introducing him to the wonderful baptismal waters at this historic church in the middle of East Harlem, New York.

10
Aspects of an Exemplary Ministry

Acts 20:17-38
Sermon preached on July 28, 2013

From Miletus [Paul] sent a message to Ephesus, asking the elders of the church to meet him. When they came to him, he said to them:

"You yourselves know how I lived among you the entire time from the first day that I set foot in Asia, serving the Lord with all humility and with tears, enduring the trials that came to me through the plots of the Jews. I did not shrink from doing anything helpful, proclaiming the message to you and teaching you publicly and from house to house, as I testified to both Jews and Greeks about repentance toward God and faith toward our Lord Jesus. And now, as a captive to the Spirit, I am on my way to Jerusalem, not knowing what will happen to me there, except that the Holy Spirit testifies to me in every city that imprisonment and persecutions are waiting for me. But I do not count my life of any value to myself, if only I may finish my course and the ministry that I received from the Lord Jesus, to testify to the good news of God's grace.—Acts 20:17-24

I majored in history in college, with a concentration in American history. Among what I remember studying were great speeches by

74

various luminaries. For example, we studied George Washington's "Farewell Speech," in which he decided to leave the presidency even though he could easily have been reelected. As the first-ever US president, he judged that it was better to leave so another could serve and the US presidency would not be interpreted as a perpetual monarchy.

More than sixty years later, Abraham Lincoln delivered his famous "Gettysburg Address" on a Civil War battlefield in Pennsylvania, when the suffering and death from the war was beyond measure on both sides. Lincoln lamented the deaths but also knew such sacrifice was needed to preserve the unity of the nation and eliminate the scourge of slavery.

In 1961 John F. Kennedy's inaugural address as president challenged his listeners "to ask not what your country can do for you—ask what you can do for our country." This was as clear and precise a call to service as has ever been heard from a US president.

Two years later, in August 1963, a non-president, Martin Luther King Jr., sounded another stirring call to the nation before throngs gathered at the Washington Monument. He proclaimed his great dream of ending racial division in the United States. With emphasis "not on the color of your skin but the content of your character," he proclaimed, "I have a dream today!"

These are all great and important speeches in the history of this nation. The Book of Acts has a few important speeches as well, including two we have explored in this sermon series— Peter's in Acts 2 and Stephen's in Acts 7. Here in Acts 20 we have another. Paul says goodbye to his ministry and to his ministry partners in Ephesus with a great speech, which I want to discuss with you this morning. Some of the key points in that speech, I think, help us learn some aspects of an exemplary ministry, both Paul's back then and what we need in leadership today.

Character, Message, and Calling (Acts 20:17-24)

Paul recognizes that part of his success among the Ephesians and all his congregations in Asia and Greece had been due to his *integrity of character*, including how he behaved with them, his service and humility, and his willingness to confront difficulties in the ministry, even when tears were needed.

Then Paul *emphasizes his message*—"proclaiming the message to you and teaching you publicly and from house to house, as I testified to both Jews and Greeks about repentance toward God and faith toward our Lord Jesus" (20:20-21). In ministry, sharing one's message as clearly as possible is very important. For Paul, bringing people to the personal knowledge of faith in Jesus as the Christ was his mission in life. Like him, we have to provide opportunities and pray to let the Holy Spirit bring people to repentance, to an "about face," a "turn around" from sin, in order to face God as revealed in Christ Jesus. Paul proclaimed these truths in synagogues, in public places for all to hear, and in homes for families to respond. Similarly, church, community, and home are the spaces we occupy in ministry in order to proclaim—in word and deed—the good news about Jesus the Christ.

Next Paul *responds to God's call* wherever it leads him (20:22-24). In his Ephesian speech, Paul acknowledges that he has to go to Jerusalem, and that perhaps he cannot expect anything good there, but rather trouble and resistance to his ministry. However, Paul has a call on his life and therefore declares with certainty and courage: "I do not count my life of any value to myself, if only I may finish my course and the ministry that I received from the Lord Jesus, to testify to the good news of God's grace" (20:24).

What gave value to Paul's life, he declares, is finishing his career in ministry with joy and accomplishing the call he received from God to bear witness to the gospel of Jesus Christ and the grace of God. What is the career God has given you—considering your "secular" career as well as your voluntary service to the church? Or maybe you are considering full-time service to God in ministry, pastoral or otherwise. Be that as it may, God has given us all a "career"—a calling, a vocation—to bear witness to the gospel of the grace of God.

Each of those words is important: we are *witnesses* that God has provided *good news*—not bad, not negative, but a positive, uplifting message, because it is *God's grace* that we represent with our lives and proclaim with our words, God's unmerited favor toward all humanity. The truth of the matter is that most of us have difficulty forgiving those who do us harm, but God does not have that problem. God's mercy, love, forgiveness, and grace have no measure. We humans need to measure things to make sure they fit us well before we invest in them, but God's grace has no measure! God goes full out to invest in human well-being.

When you recognize that your call and message—wherever and whatever they are specifically—have to do with the undeserved grace of God, you will respond like Paul: "Where do I have to go?" It may not be the safest place, the surest bet, but if God is in the matter, you'll say, "I'm going!"

The Outcome of Loyalty in Ministry (Acts 20:25-31)

Paul says farewell to his parishioners in Asia, and does so with a clear conscience. He did the work he had promised to do among them. First, he asserts that he declared to them "the whole counsel of God" (v. 26, RSV), that is, he preached what God wanted him to preach in their midst, the "will" or "purpose" of God. In other words, Paul had put it all on the table, all on the line, no holds barred. Everything he had to teach, he taught. Whatever God asked him to do, he did. How good it is when each of us can say that we tried to do our best and did so with the help of God.

Paul hopes that his work will not be in vain and that other people will take responsibility for what he needs to leave behind. In this farewell speech in Ephesus, Luke tells us that Paul addresses specifically the elders of the church whom Paul is leaving in charge with a mission. He admonishes them, "Keep watch over yourselves and over all the flock, of which the Holy Spirit has made you over-seers [*episkopoi*—"bishops, "superintendents"], to shepherd the church of God that he obtained with the blood of his own Son" (20:28). It is these "bishops"—superintendents of the mission—whose work it is to tend the church of God, to take care of it, espe-cially against "savage wolves" who do not forgive the errors of the flock but want to destroy them for anything (20:29). Even internal-ly, Paul says, it is possible that people will arise "distorting the truth in order to entice the disciples to follow them" (20:30). There are those who draw followers of Jesus with their own personal ideas and whims and for their own personal purposes and agendas that do not benefit the community of faith as a whole.

We need to pray in the spirit of Paul, "Help us, dear God, to be faithful to the message of the love and grace of Jesus Christ." Let us remember the efforts of our ancestors in Second Baptist Church and in other communities of faith to grow a faithful and strong church. Let us take care of one another so as not to fall into the temptation to destroy what God has established here. Look at Paul's plea in verse 31: "Therefore be alert, remembering that for three years I did not cease night or day to warn everyone with tears." Many a tear has been shed for Second Church for more than eighty years! Let us continue to work hard to grow and nour-ish God's church in this corner of New York City.

Finally, Take Care of the Neediest among You
(Acts 20:32-38)

Paul's last words in this stirring farewell address in Ephesus two millennia ago were about "inheritance," what he was leaving behind spiritually to those whom he had served: "And now I com-mend you to God and to the message of his grace, a message that is able to build you up and to give you the inheritance among all who are sanctified" (20:32).

Financially, Paul had practiced integrity. He was not leaving this work in Asia and Greece as a rich man. In many instances, he would rather have taken "secular" work—he writes, "I worked with my own hands"—in order not to be charged with financially exploiting the mission in Asia, which had many poor churches (20:33-34). This does not mean that many of these churches did not support Paul financially. They did. But just in case, he clarifies, he worked "with his hands" as well. He even used that opportunity in the workplace to win believers for Christ.

In fact, Paul indicates that he would rather provide financial support to needy people before he did so for himself because, citing Jesus, "It is more blessed to give than to receive" (20:35). For Paul, and for us too, there is much joy in being able to help the poor and the needy. To the extent that we can, and oftentimes in sacrificial ways, we should make available our resources from working to help those who have less, whether we do it through supporting church programs or other nonprofit agencies that serve the poor in our city, or both. And some of us will have spiritual vocations that serve the poor directly, whether in teaching ministry, social service, or other outreach services. Whether we are serving the church directly or indirectly, our service to the poor with our financial resources is a critical part of our mission and vocation as believers.

Paul concludes his farewell address with prayer (20:36-38). There was much prayer and lamentation at his departure. But it is instructive that the last thing Paul wants to do with his leaders in Ephesus is pray. Yes, they cry and lament because Paul is leaving and he has declared that they won't see him again. Yet the last memory he wants them to have of this time with them was that they prayed together. Prayer is the best resolution to a difficult time. Prayer relieves us and gives us confidence because we know that whatever happens, we are not alone. God, and our brothers and sisters, are with us.

Conclusion

My departure after this morning, of course, is not as dramatic as Paul's. After all, I am just going on vacation for a couple of weeks. Moreover, even as I go on vacation, I know the church is in good hands. Nonetheless, farewells, even temporary ones, are sad. However, they are also opportunities for others to step in, serve and help, and in that way, grow. The elders of the churches in Ephesus and Asia were sad because Paul was going and perhaps they would not see him anymore because he had plans to go to Jerusalem and then to Rome. Nonetheless, "if God is for us, who is against us?" (Romans 8:31).

We must depend on the almighty God to take care of us and we must move forward no matter what happens. That is the case for Second Baptist Church in a larger sense since you are in between settled pastors at this stage in your history. You said goodbye to a twenty-year pastorate after you said goodbye to a thirty-year pastorate. Transitions are not in any case easy. But with the help of God and the vigilance of our leaders, the church moves forward, now and forever, with character and integrity, with a message of good news, with a sense of calling and confidence, and with prayer—much prayer. How many can say amen to that? Amen!

> **Prayer:** *Dear God, goodbyes are never easy. Yet they give us an opportunity to take stock of where we have been and where we are going. Second Baptist Church is going through transition and will need to evaluate our next steps in terms of pastoral leadership and what the future holds. Bless the church as we think carefully about the direction we are headed, even as we consider where we have been as a church and what new avenues of ministry you have for us. Thank you for the leadership that has served this church so well and the leadership now in*

place to continue to guide the church's ministry and future. In Christ's name we pray. Amen!

Two Personal Notes on This Sermon: American History and Next Steps in Preaching / First, this last sermon in the series on Acts included an opening that featured great speeches from American history, including George Washington's "Farewell Address." The heart of the sermon was looking at another famous "farewell address," from Paul at Ephesus in Acts 20. Some might question referencing American history in a Latino/a church. I do not. After all, Latino/as have been an integral part of American history for centuries. Indeed, it was under a Spanish flag that Columbus led his expedition across the Atlantic. Moreover, children and youth in the church study American history in their schools. They, as well as their parents, who have lived it, should make the connections from the apostle Paul to Washington, Lincoln, Kennedy, and King, to us. Of course this assumes that here and in other sermons the preacher makes connections to specifically Latino and Latina luminaries and histories, as well as the day-to-day lives of the Latinas and Latinos who occupy the pews of this church. This I have tried to indicate in sermons reproduced throughout this volume and throughout my preaching efforts at Second Spanish Baptist Church in 2013.

Second, this was the closing sermon of a summer series on the Book of Acts that took us from the beginnings of the Christian church at Pentecost with the coming of the Spirit (Acts 2) to the beginnings of a diverse leadership for that church as described in Acts 6 to the transitions that church went through from being mostly Jewish to broadly Greco-Roman in Acts 10. Paul's ministry, which occupies the entire second half of Acts, was highlighted in sermons about the coming of the Spirit to new groups of disciples in Acts 19 and Paul's farewell address to ministry in Asia and Greece in preparation for final ministries in Jerusalem and Rome.

Throughout this summer series, my hope was for the modern-day version of Christ's church, in the life of Second Baptist Church, a church in transition, to see the connections of Spirit, leadership, and change from ancient to current day in their own lives as a community of lively faith and a hopeful tomorrow. After time off, my plan was to come back in the fall with a series on the importance of acknowledging this church's rich history and teaching it to a new generation of young believers.

Part Three

Education and History
in the Church

Until this time in my preaching at Second Spanish Baptist Church of New York, I had focused on sermons from two main books of the New Testament, Philippians and Acts, both with the goal of painting for this contemporary church in transition a picture of the ancient Christian church with their beginning triumphs, struggles, and transitions. For the remainder of my preaching time with Second Church, however, from September through my departure in early January, I relied on readings from the Revised Common Lectionary to identify and structure my sermons. This was not a church, as far as I could tell, who was accustomed to lectionary preaching. I had grown to appreciate that resource over the years of on-and-off preaching in more liturgical settings, such as the United Church of Christ. It gave me ready-made texts and materials from which I could shape the message that I thought the church needed to hear, even as I was employing previously selected texts that many Protestant churches were using around the world at the same time.

So that's what I did starting in September 2013, even though, given the seasons of the church calendar, both liturgical and event-wise locally, I knew I had to preach about certain themes: Christian education (as a new season of Sunday school programs was beginning), church history (as Second Baptist Church was celebrating their eighty-fifth anniversary in October), and, of course, Thanksgiving and Christmas. Interestingly, when I looked up the lectionary texts on the UCC website for worship resources, the readings were a bit obscure for my taste, frankly. In September and October, the Pastoral Epistles (1–2 Timothy and Titus) were the New Testament epistle readings. For Advent and Christmas, the main texts were from the prophet Isaiah. Neither of these would have been my first choices. Nonetheless, I forged ahead with my commitment to "preach from the lectionary" to see where that would take us.

11
The Church's Educational Ministry: What We Teach

1 Timothy 1:12-16
Sermon preached on September 15, 2013

I am grateful to Christ Jesus our Lord, who has strengthened me, because he judged me faithful and appointed me to his service, even though I was formerly a blasphemer, a persecutor, and a man of violence. But I received mercy because I had acted ignorantly in unbelief, and the grace of our Lord overflowed for me with the faith and love that are in Christ Jesus. The saying is sure and worthy of full acceptance, that Christ Jesus came into the world to save sinners—of whom I am the foremost. But for that very reason I received mercy, so that in me, as the foremost, Jesus Christ might display the utmost patience, making me an example to those who would come to believe in him for eternal life.
—1 Timothy 1:12-16

With this sermon, I begin a series of three messages on the church's educational ministry. A new season of Sunday school classes has begun, and our children begin a new school year in their weekly education experience outside home and church. So there is much to pray about and think about in terms of our responsibilities as educators of our church and families. These sermons are based on passages in letters known as 1 and 2 Timothy, in which tradition holds that the apostle Paul wrote instructions to the church in Ephesus and its leaders.

For this first sermon, I have cited a passage that teaches us about what we believe and therefore teach. Let us explore, therefore, these aspects of our faith and doctrines.

Called to Service by God's Mercy
(1 Timothy 1:12-14)

God strengthens us, helps us to be faithful, and gives us ministry. This includes you, teachers of the church. Even though we are redeemed sinners (v. 13), according to these words in 1 Timothy, what we did in the past was because we were mired in ignorance and unbelief. That is why it is so important to counteract lack of knowledge and lack of faith by what we teach. The grace of God in Christ, asserts the author, is more abundant and powerful than ignorance and unbelief. Love and faith in Christ Jesus supersede hatred and faithlessness. If we can teach people—members and nonmembers, people of all ages—that from ignorance and unbelief we can be transformed into the faith and love of Christ by his grace and mercy, that makes for an outstanding Christian education ministry!

For that to be a reality, however, we each need a sense of calling to this ministry, including the ministry of teaching. Echoing the words of the apostle Paul in Ephesians 4:11-13, we each have a service—a *diakonia*—to provide in the name of Christ. Some, whom we celebrate today, are teachers. Others are missionaries—they do outreach in the streets of East Harlem and the Bronx. Still others are counselors in hospitals and their workplaces. Even our public school teachers who profess faith in Jesus Christ exercise a ministry among the children of our community without necessarily saying much about their faith but simply being exemplars of love and care.

The Word We Share (1 Timothy 1:15-16)

Continuing on, this passage asserts that Christ came into the world to save, which means to liberate and restore sinners like you and me who are far from God. In another context, Paul wrote, "All have sinned and fall short of the glory of God" (Romans 3:23). However, God had mercy on us. Christ showed mercy, the text says, forgiving us. Therefore we must preach and teach all people, not with condemnation, but with words of forgiveness and mercy and love and justice. These are the values and practices that will bring those who are far from God close to God.

Part of teaching is imparting good examples. In Jesus Christ we receive mercy; Jesus Christ showed mercy to each one of us, and we can live as good examples "to those who would come to believe in him for eternal life" (v. 16). The educational ministry of the church, therefore, teaches about the basics: (1) Jesus Christ came to the world to save and restore, not destroy. (2) In Christ, God showed mercy and love toward us. (3) We believe, teach, and live these realities so that we can be examples to those in need of a personal encounter with God.

Conclusion: A Personal Testimony

Second Baptist Church, let us be a church that teaches the great truths of Jesus Christ today and every day—in class, in worship, in daily life. Let us continue considering our educational ministry in the coming weeks and years. How will we structure and organize it? What will we teach, and who will teach?

You should know, dear church, that my first experience of teaching was as a Sunday school teacher in my local church growing up in Brooklyn. That would not be unusual for most of us in the church teaching ministry, except that I started very early, too early, in fact! Upon graduation from my junior Sunday school class at age fifteen, our teacher quit, and my pastor, the beloved

Rev. Miguel Angel Rivera, seeing something in me, perhaps an early calling to the teaching ministry, assigned me to teach the class from which I had just graduated. Of course, I was not very good, especially since I was teaching kids close to my own age, and while I may have known the Bible stories well, I did not necessarily know how to teach them to the young boys in that class (in those days, our Sunday school classes were divided by gender, a good thing for a novice like me). Slowly but surely I got better, and by the time I went to college, I was the youth Sunday school teacher for the high-school-age kids. Eventually, of course, teaching biblical studies and theology became my professional ministry. I will always be thankful for those early opportunities, although I still feel sorry for those kids!

Thankfully, in Second Baptist Church, we have good, experienced teachers at all levels. Today I want to pray for our children in their studies here at church and especially at school. I also want to pray for all the public school teachers and administrators we have in our church, as well as the Sunday school teachers and administrators. Come join me at the altar to receive the blessing of God in this new school year. We value the educational ministry of the church both in these four walls and outside of them. Amen!

A Prayer for Teachers and Students: *Dear God, as we begin a new school year in our Sunday school program here at church, as well as in our public school system, I pray that you bless us all—teachers, students, administrators, and parents. Help us to learn the great truths of our faith as expressed here in our biblical traditions. Help us to live out our faith in ways that give genuine testimony here in church but especially in our schools and communities, and at home. Use all of us, those who study and those who teach, to represent the faith in Jesus Christ that you have infused in us and his great*

love for us and all of humanity. For it is in his name we
pray. Amen!

A Personal Note on This Sermon: Preaching the Pastoral Epistles /
One of the theological difficulties I have in preaching from the
Pastoral Epistles (1–2 Timothy and Titus) to a fairly traditional
church is my scholarly opinion and personal conviction that the
apostle Paul did not write them. Rather, I believe his followers used
his teachings to instruct a new generation of Pauline believers and
congregations toward the end of the first century, several years or
even decades after Paul's death. I did not take time to explain that
from the pulpit in these sermons, so you will see me using circum-
locutions ("the author wrote," etc.), or depending on the context,
my plain use of the name of Paul without suggesting that the
author wasn't the "living Paul." I determined, for good or bad, that
it would be too distracting with this congregation, and many that
I preach in, in fact, to delve into authorial issues in the Pastoral
Epistles. So I "punted," focusing on what we learn that is useful for
our faith and church life today from these ancient pseudonymous
writings that belong to our Christian New Testament canon.

As this was the first Sunday of a new Sunday school year, there
were other program items in the service, introducing the teachers
and the classes, and making announcements about the themes for
the year, which the Sunday school superintendents (for children
and adults) led. I kept my sermon somewhat briefer than most and
focused on the tasks of teaching the basics of the faith and on offering prayers for our teachers and students.

12
The Truth of the Gospel
in the Educational Ministry
of the Church

1 Timothy 2:1-7
Sermon preached on September 22, 2013

First of all, then, I urge that supplications, prayers, intercessions, and thanksgivings be made for everyone, for
kings and all who are in high positions, so that we may
lead a quiet and peaceable life in all godliness and dignity. This is right and is acceptable in the sight of God our
Savior, who desires everyone to be saved and to come to
the knowledge of the truth.
For
    there is one God;
      there is also one mediator
           between God and
           humankind,
    Christ Jesus, himself human,
      who gave himself a ransom for
           all
—this was attested at the right time. For this I was
appointed a herald and an apostle (I am telling the truth,
I am not lying), a teacher of the Gentiles in faith and
truth.—1 Timothy 2:1-7

We begin our reflection today with the last verse of this passage: "For this I was appointed a herald [a preacher] and an apostle [a missionary] (I am telling the truth, I am not lying), a teacher of the Gentiles in faith and truth." Many of you might say, "Pastor, I am not a preacher, an apostle, or a teacher, so I am going to take a nap while you preach." Well, wait a moment. Don't you want to know what the responsibilities are of preachers, apostles (missionaries), and teachers? In that way you can make a proper evaluation of how we are doing. Some of you will remember Mayor Ed Koch in the 1980s always asking the citizens of New York City, "How'm I doin'?" Here's a chance to have some criteria to see how I am doing as your preacher and teacher.

There is, however, "more method to my madness" this morning. I believe that some of you, or maybe many of you, even if you do not believe or accept it, may be called to be a preacher, missionary, or teacher. Certainly I want you in the congregation who are already teachers and preachers and outreach workers ("apostles," "missionaries") to pay heed to what this passage indicates is part and parcel of our work together as leaders of the church. Therefore, listen well to see that we might learn together.

In addition, I want to remind you that it is "the truth of the gospel" that we preach, share, and teach. This passage indicates the content of what needs to be preached, shared, and taught to people inside and outside the faith, the truth that we believe here in Second Baptist Church. And that truth is to be found in Christ. So let us listen for the truth that Christ wants us to live and share.

Prayer (1 Timothy 2:1)

First, the truth of the gospel is to be shared in a spirit of prayer. Without prayer, the mind cannot be clear enough to hear God speaking to us and to respond to God's call in our lives. Sometimes in our prayers we implore God to act immediately. This brings to mind the powerful statue known as *La Rogatoria* on the Paseo de la Princesa in old San Juan, Puerto Rico. It is based on a legendary story that the bishop of San Juan prayed in the harbor with the women of the city as they pleaded to God for protection from a British invasion of the Spanish colony in the nineteenth century. The story goes that the powerful British armada, thinking that the torchlights the women were holding up as they prayed indicated more soldiers than they could handle, sailed away. But the magnificent statue now there on the harbor plaza, with the women surrounding the bishop and pleading with God to act soon because the people of San Juan needed immediate action before destruction, indicates that it was a prayer of supplication to God and was what secured the city's survival. Similarly, we read in 1 Timothy 2 that we should offer prayers of supplication to God for immediate response in times of crisis.

Yet most times our prayers consist of continual petitions before God until God answers, sometimes after a period of time. These are the "prayers and intercessions" that take up most of our prayer time. Faithfulness and patience are key. And this passage teaches that we always pray with an attitude of thanks to God, whatever happens and however long it takes, because we know that God knows better than us what we need at any given moment.

Kings (1 Timothy 2:2)

The biblical author also asks his parishioners to pray "for kings and all who are in high positions, so that we may lead a quiet and peaceable life in all godliness and dignity." In a context of oppression in the Roman Empire, the church is urged to keep the authorities in prayer so that they might act with justice and dignity. Today we who live in a democracy want our political leaders and government officials to act justly for all our people.

The Bible consistently asks for prayer for political and religious leaders. We do not expect them always to be the best people in the world, but as long as they are fair and upright with their responsibilities, they merit our prayers and support. Otherwise, we can—and must—voice our resistance and displeasure, and the next time we have an opportunity, vote them out of office. God help us in the upcoming mayoral elections in New York City to do the right thing for our fellow citizens. Do not stop voting and, above all, do not stop praying that God will provide us with just, compassionate, and competent leaders.

Why? Because this is "right and is acceptable in the sight of God," we read in 1 Timothy 2:3. We pray for our leaders, religious and political, because we need righteous and honest leaders in positions of authority. They should want us to live "quiet and peaceable" lives with "godliness and dignity," and indeed help us work toward that end! When there is tranquility and security in society, its members can live and thrive in peace. In particular, people of faith can practice what they believe in freedom, including, as Christians, sharing the good news of Christ.

We mourn today the tragedy of shootings in Nairobi, Kenya, yesterday, where sixty-seven innocent people lost their lives in a mall at the hands of four gunmen who also died in the ensuing gun battle and fire. Religious and political unrest in that country set the stage for this horrific event.[1] However, we do not have to go so very far away to find trouble, because this week in Washington, DC, twelve innocent people were shot to death in a naval facility by a mentally ill former sailor.[2] Lord, have mercy!

We pray that God brings peace and tranquility to governments and people around the world. May God always help us to be purveyors of peace in a world that all too often confronts sad and horrible violence.

God (1 Timothy 2:3-5)

God desires such peace for the world. In this passage we learn more about the nature of God, an integral part of the truth of the gospel that we proclaim and teach. God wants "everyone to be saved and to come to the knowledge of the truth" (2:4). Everyone within our reach, within reach of this church, should have the opportunity to hear about God, because God loves everyone. We serve a God of universal love, and we are called to invite every person to know God more closely.

One reality people should understand about God, argues the author of this passage, is that "there is one God; there is also one mediator between God and humankind" (2:5). The singular God has provided, as proof of God's love for all of creation, a "mediator" who stands between our sin and estrangement from God and the possibility of eternal salvation—rescue—from that estrangement for all humanity. The mediator is Jesus Christ, whose role it is to close the distance between God and alienated humanity. Such teaching should be core to our Christian educational programs.

Christ (1 Timothy 2:5-6)

How else is Christ described? Because Christ is our mediator, we are not alone or without a lawyer. Christ intercedes for us. This Christ is also "Christ Jesus, himself human" (v. 5). Thus the Jesus of history is described here, Jesus of Nazareth, who lived as a human being among humans, shared and taught the love of God with his fellow human beings, and died as a man as a result of his demonstration of love. We do not serve a Christ who does not understand us in our humanity. It is Jesus, the fellow human, and also Jesus the Christ, anointed special envoy of God who rose from the dead and was exalted by God.

We have the best of both worlds—the God of love, who sent us Christ, who knows what it is like to be human. Christ is also a sacrificial Christ, "who gave himself [as] a ransom for all" (2:6) and thus became our rescuer from the power of sin and eternal death. This Christ continues to bear witness to his love and kindness day after day in our lives.

Conclusion

Therefore I want to continue preaching and teaching about the love and kindness of Jesus the Christ, whether from a pulpit as a preacher or in the classroom as a teacher. The educational ministry of the church is to proclaim in word and deed the love of God in Christ.

Do you feel the call of God in your life to be someone who, in one form or another, preaches, teaches, and otherwise testifies to the truth of the gospel in good times and bad times? I think about the great New York Yankees relief pitcher Mariano Rivera. His athletic career has been marked by one great skill—the ability to throw a fastball that cut into the left-handed batter and away from the right-handed hitter at the last moment, so that the hitter would almost always miss it or hit it badly into an out. With that one single pitch, one unique athletic truth, Mariano Rivera had a fabulous career that celebrates its end this year, 2013. He also has another, more important truth in his life—the truth of the gospel. Mariano Rivera has been a man of faith, and in his retirement he and his wife, Clara, will dedicate themselves to the gospel ministry, establishing churches here in the US and in their homeland, Panama.

The question before us today as a church and as individual believers, and as we consider what lies at the heart of our Christian education ministry is this: Are we willing to devote ourselves to the truth of the gospel of Jesus Christ with our preaching, our sense of mission, and our clear and accurate teaching about God and Christ? I think we are. Amen!

Prayer: *May the God of peace, love, and care, who sent us Jesus the Christ to show us the way of faith, even in sacrifice, guide us each and every day in our teaching and preaching, and especially in bearing witness of God's love to a needy world. Amen!*

A Personal Note on This Sermon: Violence Continues / As I look back on this sermon and its reference to violent events of that week I preached it (in September 2013), I am saddened to think about how much more violence we have seen in the years since: police shootings of unarmed black men, mass shootings in schools, night-clubs, and public squares, both in the US and abroad. When I preached this sermon, pleading for prayers for our government leaders and for concrete action in light of such violence and unrest, we were about to be a year removed from the tragic Sandy Hook Elementary school shootings in Newtown, Connecticut (December 2012), about an hour from my home in West Hartford, which impacted our state so much. New gun control laws were enacted statewide as a result, but not nationwide, and still the violence continues to this day. So when I cited 1 Timothy's exhortation for the church to pray "for kings and all who are in high positions, so that we may lead a quiet and peaceable life in all godliness and dignity" as part of our educational ministry, the exhortation is true now more than ever. Indeed, as we have seen after the horrific Parkland, Florida, school shootings (Valentine's Day 2018), young people in particular demand action from our political leaders in support of the "quiet and peaceable life" this text calls for us all.

Notes
1. "Gunmen Kill Dozens in Terror Attack in Kenyan Mall," *New York Times*, September 21, 2013.
2. "Gunman and Twelve Victims Killed in Shooting at D.C. Navy Yard," *New York Times*, September 16, 2013.

13
Life and Testimony in the Church's Educational Ministry

1 Timothy 6:11-19
Sermon preached on September 29, 2013

As for those who in the present age are rich, command them not to be haughty, or to set their hopes on the uncertainty of riches, but rather on God who richly provides us with everything for our enjoyment. They are to do good, to be rich in good works, generous, and ready to share, thus storing up for themselves the treasure of a good foundation for the future, so that they may take hold of the life that really is life.—1 Timothy 6:17-19

What values should we promote in our Christian educational ministry, whether in Sunday school, Bible studies, or preaching? First Timothy ends with some very pertinent suggestions. Let us discuss some in our reflection this morning, reminding us that we are seeking guidance for our ministry of Christian education in the church as we begin our new fall season of teaching ministry to children, youth, and adults.

Exhortation to the Leader (1 Timothy 6:11-12)

First, the leader must flee from evil. Later in this sermon, when I talk about the end of the passage, I will elaborate on what comes before this text with regard to the specific matters that are to be fled, in particular the misuse of wealth. But as our lectionary passage begins, the writer discusses what is more important, a positive exhortation. What should the leader, including the educational leader, pursue? The passage cites the values of justice, piety, faith, love, patience, and meekness.

Like many of you who drive a lot, I have always liked a good map of how to get to places. We are now all spoiled with our global positioning systems, our GPSs. We just type in an address, make the correct turns, and soon we arrive. This list of values in 1 Timothy 6:11-12 consists of attitudes and practices that we follow, and they are more like landmarks on a map than turn-by-turn directions from a GPS. We can be successful in life in much that we undertake by following lists of values like these.

The list includes *justice*—doing right for all; *piety*—attention to our spiritual life with God; *faith*—trust that God can and will work on our behalf; *love*—care and concern for someone other than ourselves; *patience*—waiting and trusting, even when things don't look good. Just keep on waiting. God will act. Be patient. God will step in with someone to help. The solution to the problem will come on time.

And perhaps my favorite value in this list, though not the easiest, is *meekness*—gentleness. I know that in New York City we have to be tough. Do you all know the story of the bilingual cat? Once in New York, a mouse was running from a cat. The mouse hid in a hole, trying to wait out the cat. Before long the mouse heard a dog barking and figured he was safe (although we know in the real world dogs eat mice too, but bear with me for a moment!). When the mouse stuck out his head figuring he could outrun a dog, the cat was there ready to pounce and devour his victim. As the cat got ready to eat the mouse, he explained, "In this city, you have to be bilingual!"

In this city, you have to be tough so you won't get "eaten alive." But I still think a little gentleness and a little kindness can go a long way. Doing things faithfully and confidently with each other, believing the best of our brothers and sisters, treating one another with affection, patience, and without a tongue that cuts, but rather one that comforts and rejoices, are not bad values to have, even in this tough city!

The author of 1 Timothy asks the church leader to fight "the good fight of the faith" (6:12). Church leaders, including Christian educators, should look forward to the eternal life that awaits us, to which we are called to commence one day and to which each of us has responded with a profession of faith (6:12). A good start deserves a good ending, but we must continually struggle against the winds and tides that do battle against a good ending. We are in a battle of faith on our way toward the eternal life promised by God. Practicing the values of justice, piety, faith, love, patience, and meekness helps us fight a good battle.

Reminder of the God and Christ Whom We Confess (1 Timothy 6:13-16)

Every pastor, teacher, or lay leader must remember the God and Christ we serve—the God who gives us life, and Christ, the one who gave testimony of this God, even to Pontius Pilate, who was about to have Jesus killed (6:13). This God commanded us to love God and our neighbor (6:14); this Christ seeks out his faithful again and again, especially in our hour of need. We cannot teach without these basic reminders: Who is God? God is the one who gives us life. Who is Christ? Christ is the one who came for us once and will be made "manifest" again in glory. Christ is the one whom God has made "blessed and [the] only Sovereign, the King of kings and Lord of lords" (6:15).

In our Christian education program, an understanding of Christ, his titles in texts like these, and God's sovereignty as reflected in Christ are all worth exploring. To Christ, this text teaches, is owed honor and eternal praise (6:16). God, as reflected in Christ, is immortal, an inaccessible light. But although we cannot see God in all of God's glory, we do feel God in the deepest of our hearts and in divine manifestations among us each and every day.

It is my conviction, and I think yours as well, that the church's educational ministry is dedicated to teaching and bringing light and understanding to this Christ. How many can say amen to that?

The Challenge of Riches (1 Timothy 6:17-19)

Our educational responsibilities as a church are not without challenges. Among the many challenges that exist to finish our race of faith, says 1 Timothy 6, is the challenge of riches. Remember that at the beginning of this passage, the writer urges leaders—whether teachers, pastors, or believers in general—to "shun all [evil]" (6:11). Well, one of the things to flee is anxiety over money.

In the verses before this week's lectionary reading (see 1 Timothy 6:6-10), the author points out how some choose the path of financial gain over the positive benefits of piety, a spirituality that includes contentment with what we have, that is, in terms of sustenance and shelter (6:6-8). Sometimes the pursuit of money and financial gain at all costs can lead to spiritual bankruptcy, "ruin and destruction" as the author writes (6:9). The infamous dictum "Money is the root of all evil" is not actually what the text says. Rather, it is "the love of money" that can create or be at the "root of all kinds of evil" (6:10). People can fall into the traps of temptation and foolish greed that the exorbitant focus on accumulating money can bring. Having money—even significant riches—is of itself not bad. It is the love of money over against all else that creates deep and abiding problems.

I had an uncle who, my dad, his brother, used to tell me, was from childhood good at business. Tio Manuel knew how to make a little money selling small items in his hometown in Puerto Rico. And one day he earned enough to come to the US. He kept working hard at what he knew best, which was selling. Soon he had his own furniture and jewelry stores on Atlantic Avenue in Brooklyn, prime properties even in the 1960s and '70s. But he could not control his habits of overdrinking, having affairs outside of marriage, and foolishly throwing away his money. Eventually he lost everything, including his family. Nevertheless, he had this talent for making money (just not keeping it!). He knew how to win people over and do business. (He even had talking parrots outside his shops, trained to draw people in to buy his furniture!) There is nothing wrong with such gifts, as long as we don't let creating wealth control our lives to the detriment of everything else that we value in life, such as our family, our health, our God. (Tio Manuel came to grips with the mistakes he had made earlier in his life, and when I visited him toward the end of his days, he was more at peace, having reconciled with his adult children. He was living a quiet and modest life in a lower level of a Brooklyn brownstone, with his children and grandchildren on the upper floors. He had retired from running a candy store—a salesman to the end!)

Therefore, the biblical author gives advice in 1 Timothy 6:17-19 that we should enjoy whatever financial success we achieve by placing it in the hands of God, the one who gives life. The rich can do good things with their riches. Indeed, we need wealthy people to use their wealth for good. Real treasure will come to us when we receive eternal life, as this author asserts.

I work in a building—the Interchurch Center of New York at 475 Riverside Drive—where many religious and other types of agencies have offices and from where much good is done for society. Much of the money to build that facility was donated by John D. Rockefeller Jr., whose father was the first in a long line of a rich family that made billions in oil but also gave much of his money away to do some good in this world. They weren't perfect people by any means, but they also didn't squander their wealth on evil things. Nearby, Rockefeller also helped build a church in the 1920s for one of his favorite preachers, Henry Emerson Fosdick, who was the first pastor of the famous Riverside Church. Up the street from Riverside

Church is another Rockefeller-funded building, the International House, which provides housing for international students from around the world who come to study in New York City. These are good things that a well-to-do family did with their riches.

As 1 Timothy indicates, those who acquire riches "are to do good, to be rich in good works, generous, and ready to share" (6:18). The children of John D. Rockefeller Jr. even set up a scholarship fund for theological studies, originally known as the Rockefeller Brothers, later known as the Fund for Theological Education, to help theology students fund their seminary education. I was a recipient of those funds for part of my seminary education in the early 1980s. So we learn from these Scriptures not that money is bad, but that it is what we do with our money, a little or a lot, that can be pleasing—or not—to God. Christian education should teach, among many things, to use our possessions, whether we are rich or not, for good causes. The missionary offering that we collect today for the causes of Christ's work is an example of the historically good Christian education that this church has carried on for years!

Conclusion

The church's educational ministry is dedicated to teaching the values of our faith. It helps us to confess the life-giving God and the Christ who gave his life so that we may have eternal life. And it teaches us to be faithful in the use of our talents, time, and treasure for the glory of God, our eternal Creator, and our beloved Savior, Jesus the Christ. Amen!

> **Prayer:** *Dear God, we want to be purveyors of the faith; we want to teach about you, Christ, and the Spirit to new generations of believers so that your name is glorified. We want to live our lives faithfully, justly, and wisely. Help us, dear God, to organize and teach through an*

*educational ministry in our church that bears witness to
your love and glory. Amen!*

A Personal Note on This Sermon: "The Godbox" / My reference
to the Interchurch Center, 475 Riverside Drive, also known as "the
Godbox," in this sermon brought to mind that I first encountered
this building when I was an instructor at Boricua College in 1982.
I brought a group of my students on a field trip as part of my
Religious Studies class, so that they could see the social justice arm
of many religious bodies in action.

Originally the Interchurch Center was built (the building opened
in 1958) to house the national headquarters of many mainline
Protestant Churches, including Presbyterian, Methodist, Congregational, Baptist, Reformed, and Orthodox bodies (hence the nickname "the Godbox"). Eventually many moved their national headquarters elsewhere (e.g., Presbyterian Church, USA, to Louisville,
Kentucky; United Methodist Church to Nashville, Tennessee; United
Church of Christ to Cleveland, Ohio; etc.). A handful of auxiliary
agencies of these denominations stayed behind, and other religious,
nonprofit, social justice, and educational agencies moved in.

New York Theological Seminary, my place of employment,
moved its administrative and faculty offices there in the early 2000s
from elsewhere in the city. When I joined the faculty of NYTS in
2011, I remembered that rich legacy of this Rockefeller-funded
facility that I had first explored in 1982.

The Metro New York Association of the American Baptist
Churches also has its offices on the fourth floor of the Interchurch
Center, one flight below NYTS. Soon after my arrival at NYTS, I
met the Reverend Dr. Isaac Castañeda, associate regional minister,
with particular charge for Latino/a churches in the region. It was
he who first approached me about doing interim ministry at
Second Spanish Baptist Church in 2013.

14

Our Legacy: Remembering Our Message about Jesus

2 Timothy 2:8-15
Sermon preached on October 6, 2013

Remember Jesus Christ, raised from the dead, a descendant of David—that is my gospel, for which I suffer hardship, even to the point of being chained like a criminal. But the word of God is not chained. Therefore I endure everything for the sake of the elect, so that they may also obtain the salvation that is in Christ Jesus, with eternal glory. The saying is sure:
If we have died with him, we will also live with him;
if we endure, we will also reign with him;
if we deny him, he will also deny us;
if we are faithless, he remains faithful—
for he cannot deny himself.
Remind them of this, and warn them before God that they are to avoid wrangling over words, which does no good but only ruins those who are listening. Do your best to present yourself to God as one approved by him, a worker who has no need to be ashamed, rightly explaining the word of truth.—2 Timothy 2:8-15

Memory is important, including the act of remembering from where we came, for this helps us determine where we are going.

Therefore, as depicted in this passage from 2 Timothy, the biblical writer (traditionally portrayed as the apostle Paul) reminds his pupil, Timothy, of the basics in the message about Jesus Christ that must be remembered. What are those teachings and histories that we have to retain as a church to make our future secure?

Jesus (2 Timothy 2:8-10)

Let us remember Jesus whom we serve. Though a descendant of kings, the text argues, he did not fail to present his body in sacrifice to humanity. This sacrifice, however, ended not with death, but with resurrection, a new life to model hope for all of us. It is in these truths that we find the root of the gospel— Jesus, life, suffering, death, and resurrection. Although Jesus suffered death, "the word of God is not chained." The love of God does not remain silent but works for our eternal salvation. Therefore, in those difficult moments that invariably come our way, let us remember Jesus—his love for humanity, his commitment toward us, even to the point of death, and his victory over death.

Faithful Message (2 Timothy 2:11-13)

Because this is a faithful, true message, like Jesus was in death and resurrection, death does not have the last word, even in our lives. Suffering is real. Yes, we have difficulty in this life, but it does not have to have the last word. We must remain faithful. We do not deny Christ because we don't want him to have to say that we denied him on that fateful judgment day. Regardless of our faith, the faithfulness of Christ is forever. Christ cannot deny the faithfulness of his work on our behalf. God does not deny God. God is God whether we are faithful or not. I hope we can be faithful—trusting in God and Christ, no matter what happens in our lives.

Faithful and Prepared Leaders (2 Timothy 2:14-15)

Remember this: we need good leaders to help us not waste time. In what sense, you ask? Words of disagreement and rancor alone do not bring us resolutions or results in church conflicts. There will always be disagreements about this or that course of action as a church. However, we must present ourselves to God and to each other carefully and consistently so that we can see more clearly God's will for our lives as individuals and as a church. God wants us to invest our time not in vain, self-serving arguments, but rather to be unashamed to use the word of truth correctly.

Let me explain: We should plan with care and diligence for the future of our church in order to seek accord with each other and approval from God. For example, let us be present as good leaders in favor of the neediest in our community. A good pastoral, diaconal, and lay leadership in general takes care of the well-being of brothers and sisters. We preach the word in good times and bad times, sometimes with words and sometimes with actions. That's how Francis of Assisi described our task as Christian believers: "Preach the gospel always; when necessary, use words."

The author of 2 Timothy insists that we "explain the word of truth" (2:15). We need to carry on and carry out from these four walls of the church the proclamation of the truth of God to a needy world. When we "explain," we clarify and we keep the Word plain and simple.

For example, I work hard to bring you a good word from God every week during my tenure with you as an interim minister. However, good preaching by one man is not enough. You need a long-term pastor who will be present with you consistently and for the long haul. You need consistent pastoral care, even though that cannot be done by one person alone. Everyone needs to chip in, especially when there is so much need for hospital visits, prayers in homes, and testimony in the streets. Those are the places where the word of truth is shared and "explained"!

Conclusion

Dear church, understand well the legacy of our message—the love and sacrifice of Jesus, our Savior. Be faithful to the message that our ancestors left us, and take them to a new generation in new and clear ways. To do that, we must present ourselves to God as faithful, worthy workers, who work hard every day in faithfulness and service. This includes being present in the lives of people in need with a spirit of careful and loving pastoral care like Jesus himself, whose message we proclaim.

Brothers and sisters, your next pastor should have these qualities—consistent *presence*, attentive *pastoral care*, well-planned and prepared biblical *preaching*. You should plan, advocate, and wait patiently for these qualities of ministry to become an integral part of the next pastoral leadership that will be yours in the near future, as it was for so many years in this church's historic legacy.

May God help us in the months ahead to be faithful to this legacy, this call, and this message. Let us remember, then, that Jesus is our example par excellence of a faithful messenger and spokesman of a true and lasting message. Amen!

> **Prayer:** *Dear God, may this congregation always be blessed with great leadership, as it has been throughout its long and storied history. May the future bring the pastoral leadership that is needed to move the congregation forward into the secure future that you have planned for them. Amen!*

Final Reflection on Preaching Christian Education and History from the Pastorals / Second Spanish Baptist Church would celebrate its eighty-fifth anniversary just a week or two after I preached this sermon on the importance of remembering our "legacy." Around that same time, I made a critical announcement that I would be leaving the church as its interim minister upon conclusion of the Christmas holidays. (Eventually I also preached the first Sunday of the New Year, because the church held its annual meeting that Sunday and I wanted to provide a final report of my experience on that occasion.)

I thought the church would be better served by an interim, or maybe even a settled pastor, who lived closer than I did. Traveling from Hartford, Connecticut, even with the church apartment that was provided, to teach at New York Theological Seminary and minister to the church on weekends was taking its toll. So shortly after this sermon in early October, I announced my departure. It actually helped the church move more quickly toward securing a permanent pastor early in 2014, rather than keeping me around longer than I needed to be.

My work on the importance of teaching and remembering our history, to which I dedicated my September and October sermons and Friday night Bible studies, had its impact, I hope. I was also careful to explore these issues with church leadership and in planning and strategy sessions with the Christian education staff in a few meetings we had. But the bulk of my contribution to this church, however, remained those Sunday morning worship services, and the care I took to show the congregation organization, thinking, planning, and good theology for my sermons. Then it was time for Thanksgiving, Advent, and Christmas, a selection of sermons for which follow in the next part of this book.

Part Four

Preaching Thanksgiving, Advent, Christmas, and a New Year

In organizing myself several months earlier for the final period of my preaching at Second Spanish Baptist Church of New York, I realized the calendar would dictate my general themes. The traditional holidays of Thanksgiving, Christmas, and New Year's would guide my selection of texts and sermons. However, I was also being guided by my decision to follow the Revised Standard Lectionary texts as the basis for my sermons. I had made that decision with regard to my early fall sermons on Christian education and history, which took me to engaging texts from the Pastoral Epistles in 1 and 2 Timothy, not among my favorite texts for preaching. However, that's what lectionary preaching does for you: it encourages preaching from texts with which one is not always familiar or not among one's "favorites."

Interestingly enough, except for the actual Christmas sermon, which took us to the Gospel of Luke, the Advent sermons leading up to Christmas came from texts in the Book of Isaiah in the Hebrew Bible. Until that time, I had preached exclusively from New Testament texts during my preaching in the interim. So I engaged the challenge of preaching Advent sermons from Isaiah's prophetic texts about patience and waiting on God for deliverance from abject situations. And I also had the opportunity at the beginning of the new year, for my final sermon as interim minister of this church, to preach a Three Kings' Day sermon for a church that did not seem to practice that celebration as a matter of Sunday morning worship. These were the unique challenges I encountered in the final trimester of my service to Second Spanish Baptist Church of New York.

109

15
Gratitude for New Beginnings:
A Thanksgiving Sermon

Isaiah 65:17-25
Sermon preached on November 7, 2013

> For I am about to create new heavens
> and a new earth;
> the former things shall not be remembered
> or come to mind.
> But be glad and rejoice forever
> in what I am creating;
> for I am about to create Jerusalem as a joy,
> and its people as a delight.—Isaiah 65:17-18

This week we heard about the devastation in the Philippines caused by Typhoon Haiyan. Yesterday I read in the newspaper about a family there who lost their home. The only thing they found was a trophy that a young member of the family had won in a contest at her church. More than 3,500 people died as a result of this storm, with so much destruction and tragedy, and so much to do to rebuild. We hear news practically every day of one or another tragedy—violence, the child with autism lost in Queens, a man in Detroit who shot a woman dead when she came to his doorstep seeking help after her car broke down; tragedy after tragedy.

Although centuries removed, in a world where death and destruction was often even more prevalent, how is it possible that the prophet Isaiah could write so positively? "For I am about to create new heavens and a new earth; the former things shall not be remembered or come to mind. But be glad and rejoice forever in what I am creating; for I am about to create Jerusalem as a joy, and its people as a delight" (Isaiah 65:17-18).

Is it possible that from nothing—from destruction, from tragedy—you can, as God's people, believe in the power of community, of love, of peace, of hope, and of a new day? The prophet Isaiah affirms it. How could it be possible? Can we give thanks this Thanksgiving season, even when there doesn't seem a lot for which to give thanks?

The Context of Isaiah 65, in Brief

Jerusalem at the time when Isaiah 65 was written was still in ruins after the destruction by Babylon more than a hundred years before. Only a few houses and businesses, as well as the temple, had been partially rebuilt. There was much hunger, sickness, sadness, and economic injustice. But the prophets, such as Isaiah, still believed in the power of God to restore God's people and alleviate their suffering:

> I will rejoice in Jerusalem,
> and delight in my people;
> no more shall the sound of weeping be heard in it,
> or the cry of distress.
> No more shall there be in it
> an infant that lives but a few days,
> or an old person who does not live out a lifetime;
> for one who dies at a hundred years will be considered
> a youth,
> and one who falls short of a hundred will be
> considered accursed. (65:19-20)

We also see injustice in our day with children who die prematurely of diseases that can be cured, people who die young and should have long lives. Not everyone has had the blessing of our dear sister Viterba Ortiz, who has reached nearly one hundred years old![1]

For now, we all face many tears and sorrows. We believe that one day these will end when Christ comes for faithful believers. Meanwhile, we pray and work so that a glimpse of that final salvation becomes real in the lives of many people today, including the lives of many around us, both in our church and in our neighborhoods. The prophet Isaiah prayed for his people and claimed victory for them, although the evidence was not being seen in the ruins of his city. That's called faith! How does the writer of the Book of Hebrews put it? "Now faith is the assurance of things hoped for, the conviction of things not seen" (Hebrews 11:1).

To Achieve This Prophetic Vision, We Have to Work

The prophet clarifies the reality of the work necessary to achieve the hope that we should have in God. It is a lively, current hope even if we have only a glimpse of the future that we will have:

> They shall build houses and inhabit them;
> they shall plant vineyards and eat their fruit.
> They shall not build and another inhabit;
> they shall not plant and another eat;
> for like the days of a tree shall the days of my people be,
> and my chosen shall long enjoy the work of their hands.
> (65:21-22)

What a beautiful vision! The one who works should enjoy the fruits of his or her labor justly. What good is it for me to work to build and clean the houses of others if I cannot have affordable and pleasant spaces for my family? The city of New York has recently built a bad reputation for having homes that only the richest can afford. And what about those who have worked hard in this city for many years, who have raised families and made contributions to the growth of New York? Is it not fair that they, too, should have a comfortable place for their families?

Some of you might say, "Pastor, don't get into those things. That's being too political!" Actually, I am simply reading the text of Isaiah and wondering if the injustices done against the Israelites and their sufferings after their exile and return are not teachings that could help us to try and live well in the present as a testimony of what God has in store for faithful people in a future not too far away. Of course they are!

Pray and act so we might "enjoy the work of [our] hands." God wants and has the best for us, and that includes in the present. The Bread of Life ministry that we have supported as a church on Saturday mornings is an example of something we can do now for the well-being of many in our neighborhood. We need people to stand and say, "Here I am, Lord, send me." This includes the men in our church, who for the first time in a long time met on our own this past Friday evening to make plans for our ministries as men of the church. Let us all go and work in the vineyard of the Lord, including in this Saturday morning feeding program, Bread of Life, that needs to be kept alive by new leadership and engagement.

What Is the World That God Wants to Build in the Future and in the Present?

The prophet Isaiah describes it as follows:

> They shall not labor in vain,
> or bear children for calamity;
> for they shall be offspring blessed by the Lord—
> and their descendants as well.
> Before they call I will answer,
> while they are yet speaking I will hear.
> The wolf and the lamb shall feed together,
> the lion shall eat straw like the ox;

> but the serpent—its food shall be dust!
> They shall not hurt or destroy
> on all my holy mountain,
> says the LORD. (65:23-25)

God will take care of us. We need to work now as hard as we can to build our homes, our families, our communities, our church, and our city. Even if we do not see immediate positive results, God assures us that our work will not be in vain. Your efforts, dear leaders of the church and all of you brothers and sisters, are helpful now and will continue to produce good things in the future. They will certainly not be a "calamity" or a "curse," as some translations of this Isaiah text read, but a blessing. Thus says the Lord!

God is a God of good timing. Even before we cry out to God, God is attentive to our needs. The world that God wants to create is a world of peace—where wolves and lambs, lions and oxen have friendship and eat together. Imagine in your minds the worst kind of enemies in the world today, and believe and work toward one day seeing those opponents at peace with each other.

We must be in search of that peace with one another, even now in anticipation of the final peace. Christians, even if we have our differences, in the end, peace and unity is what should distinguish us in a world of conflict and violence. Nothing whatsoever, not even theological and ecclesiastical disagreements, should have us tearing one another's hair out in the church of God. "Lions" and "oxen" in communities of faith need to sit together and reach agreements for the good of the church and the good of the world that so very greatly needs us to exercise and exemplify peace and love.

This harmony is needed so that "snakes" and all that do harm in this world will one day have no place to do their evil. In the present, we try to achieve that reality, for this is the world that God wants to create, a "holy mountain," writes the prophet. We want to be part of what God is doing now and tomorrow. We want to step on that "holy mountain," that new creation, the new city of Jerusalem.

Conclusion

What do we do now until the day of a new Jerusalem? I suggest the following: First, keep up to date with news from the Philippines this week to see how we can help in their restoration after the terrible tragedy of that storm. I pray that the missionary offering we collect today in honor of Thanksgiving will be directed by our denomination to that cause.

Second, let us reopen the Bread of Life feeding ministry for at least two Saturdays a month with the help of some men who will accompany the women who have been in leadership, women who have been cooking and leading the brief worship service that is part of the feeding ministry. We want those who enter our doors with hunger to receive both physical and spiritual food.

Third, in the coming weeks, if you are approached to participate in any church ministry for this coming new year, do not refuse. Rather, be willing to serve for the glory of God and for the well-being of our church and community.

Fourth, and above all, pray for the next pastor of this church. This congregation has an important future in this community, and it takes creative, enduring, and strong leadership to move forward, creating the community of peace and love that God wants us to have in the here and now. And do all this in the spirit of the season of Thanksgiving, a spirit of gratitude.

Therefore, receive with joy, hope, and gratitude the promises of Isaiah 65:18:

> But be glad and rejoice forever
> in what I am creating;
> for I am about to create Jerusalem as a joy,
> and its people as a delight.

Segunda Iglesia Bautista, you are God's Jerusalem in the present; you are God's joy. You are the people who bring God delight. May it be so now and always! Amen!

> **Prayer:** *Dear God, may this church always find, in the Spirit of Thanksgiving for all the good you do for us, the time to do good for others. Help us to reach out in the spirit of the prophet Isaiah, who had high hopes for the restoration of his community even in the midst of destruction, to see a new Jerusalem already in some form in our neighborhoods and communities. We pray for sustenance, hope, and power to do the right thing for our communities in need, now and until Christ returns to build the eternal city of God, a city of love and justice. Amen!*

A Personal Note on This Sermon: The Bread of Life Ministries / One of the longtime social justice programs of Second Baptist Church, its Saturday morning feeding program, Pan de Vida, was suffering from lack of engagement by enough people, especially men, to keep it open. So it went on hiatus for a while, and I spent some time trying to revive it. We had a men's meeting on a Friday night in October, and that was one of the discussions. At the church's annual meeting in January, my last Sunday before I left, I proposed that at least twice a month, men and women from the church take turns opening up the church on Saturday mornings, preparing a hot breakfast, and conducting a brief worship service and prayer time, trying in that way to bear witness to the church's ongoing concern for its immediate neighborhood, including the homeless.

Note
1. On September 14, 2016, Viterba Ortiz turned one hundred years old. She has been a member of Second Baptist for seventy-five years and is a "deacon for life."

16
Waiting for Christ:
An Advent Sermon

Isaiah 2:1-5
Sermon preached on December 1, 2013

> The word that Isaiah son of Amoz saw concerning Judah
> and Jerusalem:
> In days to come
> the mountain of the LORD's house
> shall be established as the highest of the mountains,
> and shall be raised above the hills;
> all the nations shall stream to it.
> Many peoples shall come and say,
> "Come, let us go up to the mountain of the LORD,
> to the house of the God of Jacob;
> that he may teach us his ways
> and that we may walk in his paths."—Isaiah 2:1-3

This season is not about Black Friday, Cyber Monday, or Small Business Saturday (although the latter is a good idea—supporting local businesses instead of just the big stores). The season before us is Christmas, but even on these Sundays before Christmas Day arrives, the season in Christian churches is known as *Advent*.

Advent is the time to *wait* for Christ, for his birth, his visit to us for the first time, and the meaning of such a visit. Indeed, Christ visits us every day in anticipation of his *second* coming. *The present*

Christ is the focus of our celebration this month, including his gift of love and sacrifice. In fact, that is why we have the custom of giving gifts, or at least that should be our attitude in giving. We buy with love in mind, not with a fight for who gets the best deal.

Kids, when your parents give at Christmas, it is to honor Christ, the giver of life and love. So receive your gifts with love and thanksgiving, because that is the place from which they come, whatever the cost of the gift or whether you get what you really wanted. Sometimes you get it, sometimes you don't, but you always get love, which is the original gift of Christmas, the gift of sacrificial love, from Christ.

Let us prepare for this Christmas with the appropriate attitude in what we expect—the arrival of Jesus. Advent from the Latin word *adventus*—"coming" or "arrival"—recognizes the weeks leading up to Christmas as a time to develop the right attitude about the birth of Jesus. How do we prepare? This text of Isaiah, as interpreted by Christians this Advent and Christmas season, gives some guidelines of preparation for the coming of a better day, including, Christians believe, the coming of the Christ, both the first *and* the second time.

Hope (Isaiah 2:2-3)

For ancient Israel in the time of Isaiah, when the Jewish people looked at Jerusalem, their beloved city, it was all destroyed. However, the prophet Isaiah proclaimed hope for a better day, when many would be in worship in that same city. For later Christian interpreters, the holy city of Jerusalem came to prefigure and symbolize the eternal kingdom of God, which they believed Christ helped inaugurate.

> The word that Isaiah son of Amoz saw concerning Judah
> and Jerusalem:
> In days to come

the mountain of the LORD's house
shall be established as the highest of the mountains,
and shall be raised above the hills;
all the nations shall stream to it. (2:2)

Many will come to such a city one day, says the prophet. Christians claim that we wait on God, who sent us a Savior, one who died in Jerusalem. Yet such sacrifice also provided for our salvation. Therefore we always have hope even in difficult and dark times, when everything looks so desperate, because we believe that Christ is coming!

We continue to believe in Christ's daily intervention in our favor, whether in sickness, in poverty, or in any other difficulty of life. Christ always visits us, just as he did that first night of his humble birth. This is Advent hope!

Teaching (Isaiah 2:3)

The prophet tells us that when Christ comes, *we learn*! He instructs us, and we learn to walk the paths of God better.

Many peoples shall come and say,
"Come, let us go up to the mountain of the LORD,
to the house of the God of Jacob;
that he may teach us his ways
and that we may walk in his paths."
For out of Zion shall go forth instruction,
and the word of the LORD from Jerusalem." (2:3)

From Jerusalem—the place where Christ died and rose again—there is much to learn. God speaks to us through the life and ministry of Jesus. The New Testament Gospels are filled with teachings for our daily living—how to be better disciples, how to care for the needy, how to love and serve our neighbors.

In preparation for receiving the coming of Jesus this Christmas, we continue to learn all we can about his person, character, call, and instruction, and how to serve one another better as a result of those teachings. This is Advent teaching!

Peace (Isaiah 2:4)

God's promises for the days of Jesus' coming include *peace* between nations:

> He shall judge between the nations,
> and shall arbitrate for many peoples;
> they shall beat their swords into plowshares,
> and their spears into pruning hooks;
> nation shall not lift up sword against nation,
> neither shall they learn war any more. (2:4)

Instead of war, the prophet promises, there will be peace. Instead of weapons to fight with, there will be tools to sow seed for food to feed the hungry. That's why the evangelist Luke records angels singing at the birth of Christ, "Glory to God in the highest heaven, and on earth peace among whom he favors!" (Luke 2:14).

I always remember a story I heard once in relation to this Isaiah text about "learning war no more." When General Colin Powell was on the board of trustees at Howard University in Washington, DC, and chair of the university's Academic Affairs Committee, Rev. Dr. Clarence Newsome, then dean of Howard University's Divinity School, was also on that committee. General Powell asked Dean Newsome to open the committee meeting with prayer, and the dean prayed that these words from Isaiah would come true one day: "They shall beat their swords into plowshares, and their spears into pruning hooks; nation shall not lift up sword against nation, neither shall they learn war any more." Apparently the general was taken aback by this prayer, and later, as I heard Dean Newsome tell the story, asked the dean, an ordained minister, about them. How could that ever be possible—to learn war no more?

Indeed, as much as in the time of Isaiah, as in ours, one looks around and does not see much peace. Today we have war in Afghanistan, Syria, and other places. There is violence in our streets; there is turmoil in the Philippines. Where is the peace? There are glimmers of peace, with Iran perhaps, between Israel and Palestine perhaps?[1]

Certainly in the hearts of those who claim Christ as Savior, we find some inner, spiritual peace and hope. Whenever Jesus visits us and we feel his presence through the Spirit of God, we have peace, tranquility, hope, and security. Our challenge comes in sharing such peace with the world around us. But share it we must, if only with those who are closest to us: our family members, our neighbors, our coworkers. We seek peace in our church, peace in our homes, peace in our neighborhood and community. "Get to the global through the local," we have heard said over the years. "Think globally, act locally." In seminary I learned that we "get to the universal through the particular." Try to make peace with those closest to you, in the name of the Christ of Advent and Christmas. And continue to pray, like Dean Newsome did, for peace in the world. For this is the spirit of Advent peace!

Conclusion: Walking in the Light of Christ (Isaiah 2:5)

By way of summary, waiting for Christ in this Christmas season implies *walking in his light*, with all the blessings, clarity, intellect, hope, and peace that light brings. Such waiting includes learning about Jesus—his life and ministry, his teachings, his confrontation of unjust powers, and his sacrifice. This involves treating our loved ones, our colleagues at work, our neighbors, and even strangers, with love, peace, and dignity. We need to work at avoiding strife and trying to resolve it when it comes our way, in the light of Christ, the Prince of Peace.

O house of Jacob,
come, let us walk
in the light of the LORD! (2:5)

To walk in light is to let the star of Bethlehem guide us day after day until we reach the feet of the baby Jesus. Will you walk in the light this Christmas, the light of Christ, who is a light of hope, learning, and peace? Above the lights of the streets, the homes, and the Christmas trees shines the light of Christ over all that enlightens us at Christmas.

I pray to God to help us celebrate this time of waiting, of Advent, with gladness, with joy, and with peace. Buy what you need to buy, but do not fight for the bargains or spend more than you should. Go in tranquility and peace—buy, cook, celebrate, and always remember the reason for the season, the reason for this stage of our lives as a church—the Christ of peace and hope, the Christ of light. Christ is our Advent Light! Amen!

> **Prayer:** *May the God of hope, peace, and light guide your steps this Advent and Christmas season. May we all learn more about Jesus, the reason for our celebrations, the one we wait for, patiently and hopefully, loving all those who surround us, desiring your peace, dear God, for their lives. Amen.*

A Personal Note on This Sermon: A Word about Advent / As with the practice of using lectionary readings for sermons, this was not a church that seemed to employ the language of Advent for the Sundays leading up to Christmas, much like in my youth growing up in Latino/a Pentecostal churches. Once Thanksgiving happened and December started, Christmas was already in the air, and everything led in that direction, including music, plays, parties, and sermons. Liturgically, the time was Advent, but our services lacked the traditional language or candle rituals found in Advent services. If I had thought about it more, besides a few sermons invoking the tradition of Advent, like this one above, I might have tried lighting Advent candles at the beginning of the December services as well. Some of the more recent converts from Roman Catholicism might have been taken aback by my doing that, however, since it may have reminded them of Roman Catholic practices of lighting candles, including as part of prayers to saints represented by physical icons. Nonetheless, with some Bible study and discussion of Protestant models of Advent celebrations, I think eventually such candle rituals could have been a healthy addition to liturgical practices at La Segunda.

Note

1. When I first preached this, there were glimmers of hoped-for peace agreements with Iran and between Israel and Palestine, which evaporated over time, until 2015 when President Obama and his administration, along with several other countries, made agreements over nuclear arms with Iran. Ironically, as I did the final edits on this sermon for publication, on May 8, 2018, President Trump has pulled the US out of the Iran deal, creating confusion about those relationships moving forward.

17
Looking for a Place:
A Christmas Sermon

Luke 2:1-14
Sermon preached on December 22, 2013

> While they were there, the time came for her to deliver her child. And she gave birth to her firstborn son and wrapped him in bands of cloth, and laid him in a manger, because there was no place for them in the inn. —Luke 2:6-7

How beautiful are the songs of our choir with their sublime message of God's love for us in Christ Jesus, the reason for our Christmas. After hearing such beautiful music and such stirring lyrics in their songs, will we make room in our hearts for Christ Jesus?

After all of the efforts we have made this Christmas season— buying gifts, decorating our homes, sending Christmas cards, cooking *arroz con gandules y pernil* (rice with pigeon peas and roast pork), will there be room in our homes and our hearts for the baby Jesus, the reason for our Christmas?

Will There Be a Place?
Imagine, if you will, Joseph and Mary and the baby (inside Mary's womb) traveling all those miles from Nazareth to Bethlehem (from north to south, like from New York to Washington, DC), through mountains and deserts, almost all on foot, except perhaps

with a camel or donkey for Mary, if they used what little money they had. All this was undertaken just to comply with a request from the government.

> In those days a decree went out from Emperor Augustus that all the world should be registered. This was the first registration and was taken while Quirinius was governor of Syria. All went to their own towns to be registered. Joseph also went from the town of Nazareth in Galilee to Judea, to the city of David called Bethlehem, because he was descended from the house and family of David. He went to be registered with Mary, to whom he was engaged and who was expecting a child. (Luke 2:1-5)

And then, consider that when they finally arrived, there was no place to rest, no safe, clean place to have the baby. They had fulfilled all their responsibilities with the law, dutifully: "Go to your ancestral home and be registered," that is, "fill out a census form." Yet no one could or would provide a safe space for Mary to give birth.

As we know from countless retellings of the story each Christmas, the only place that was available was a stable—a none-too-hygienic or pleasant-smelling space reserved for farm animals—where this special baby would be born, the one whom we would later find out would become the Savior of the world, "because there was no place for them in the inn."

Will there be room for Jesus in a corner of our living rooms next to the Christmas tree? How about the kitchen? Did you save a *pastel*—one of your special Christmas meat pies—for Jesus, along with a bowl of rice with pigeon peas? Remember, as the song goes, "*Si me dan pasteles, demenlo caliente, porque el pastel frio emphachan la gente*" ("If you give me *pasteles*, give them to me hot, because cold *pasteles* give us indigestion!"). Do we have room for Jesus in our Christmas festivities? Brothers and sisters, let us not forget the reason for our Christmas—Jesus. Let us make room for him in our lives, in our homes, in our hearts.

Angels and Shepherds Give Glory to God

After the birth of this special child, heavenly angels visit humble shepherds tending their sheep on the slopes around Bethlehem, so that they may come to worship the humble child born in a mere manger. The shepherds are filled with fear at the sight of the angels, but they make room in their hearts for the angel's message that a humble birth will have the great impact of salvation for the whole world.

> In that region there were shepherds living in the fields, keeping watch over their flock by night. Then an angel of the Lord stood before them, and the glory of the Lord shone around them, and they were terrified. But the angel said to them, "Do not be afraid; for see—I am bringing you good news of great joy for all the people: to you is born this day in the city of David a Savior, who is the Messiah, the Lord. This will be a sign for you: you will find a child wrapped in bands of cloth and lying in a manger." And suddenly there was with the angel a multitude of the heavenly host, praising God and saying, "Glory to God in the highest heaven, and on earth peace among those whom he favors!" (Luke 2:8-14)

What irony, right? Humble shepherds are the first to recognize the one who brings peace to the world. Even in the Gospel of Matthew, it is the arrival of magi, wise counselors of pagan kings, who travel from distant places to pay homage to the child. Powerful local kings like Herod cannot believe that a child born in a manger can bring glory from the highest!

So, in the Gospel of Luke, it is heavenly angels that sing before these shepherds and for all of us centuries thereafter, "Glory to God in the highest heaven, and on earth peace among those whom he favors!" From the glorious height of God's presence comes peace and well-being for humankind through the birth, life, teachings, and sacrifices of Jesus the Christ.

Why did the angels sing this? Why did our choir sing what they did so beautifully about Jesus, and why have all of you, members and guests to our Christmas service this morning, sing so enthusiastically about Jesus and pray to him so fervently today? Would you agree with me that it is because in the baby Jesus we have the Christ of glory, even with that humble beginning? Even from that stinking stable comes peace for the earth and goodwill for all humanity.

It is good news that we proclaim this Christmas and every day of our lives. Church, our task is to proclaim good news, not bad, goodwill toward all humanity, without discrimination, so that all may experience the peace and love that emanated from that humble stable so long ago. It is good news and goodwill that we preach and live out in Jesus Christ, our Lord and Savior, just like the angels and shepherds that first Christmas two thousand years ago!

Conclusion

If this be true, then let us make room for Christ in our Christmas. Let us open the doors of our homes and our hearts. Let us sing with the heavenly angels and with the choir of the Second Baptist Church—"Glory to God in the highest, and on earth peace, good will toward [all humanity]!" (Luke 2:14, King James Version, modified). May it be thus this Christmas, all of our Christmases, and all the days of our lives. Amen!

> **Prayer:** *Help us find room, dear God, in our hearts and in our homes and in our communities for Jesus, for his love, for his care, for his peace. Can we learn from Jesus, his life and ministry, what we need to bring love and peace to a needy world? Help us, dear God, make the*

space, find the time, and share the words so that others might sing the songs of joy and peace as we have this morning. In the name of that Christ child we pray. Amen!

A Personal Note on This Sermon: An Abbreviated Christmas Sermon / At Second Spanish Baptist Church, the highlight of Christmas services was an all-out concert by the church choir. My sermon, therefore, was shorter and made reference to the choir's beautiful music. There was also a party after the service, with typical Puerto Rican and Latin American Christmas dishes in the church hall. These are established traditions, like in most Latino/a churches, like most churches in general around Christmastime. My job was to make sure all went smoothly and that my sermon, while briefer than usual, would be meaningful to the members, families, and guests gathered for the festivities.

18
Three Kings, One Star, and Great Joy: A Final Sermon

Matthew 2:1-12
Sermon preached on January 5, 2014

When they had heard the king, they set out; and there, ahead of them, went the star that they had seen at its rising, until it stopped over the place where the child was. When they saw that the star had stopped, they were overwhelmed with joy.—Matthew 2:9-10

During my upbringing in a Latino Pentecostal church, there was not much talk about the three wise men and the traditions about the Three Kings (*los Reyes Magos*) celebrated in our Latin American countries, including Puerto Rico, from where most of our families when I was growing up had come. It was my wife, Olga, born and raised in Puerto Rico, who insisted we celebrate these traditions when our children were young, and then Latino/a congregational churches we attended in Boston and later Hartford also organized celebrations around Three Kings Day in early January each year. It was only through them that I learned to celebrate the arrival of these visitors from the East to the baby Jesus. We tried to give our children a little more of these traditions on January 6 than when I was a child growing up in Brooklyn.

But several questions about our traditions always arise when reading the original story in the Gospel of Matthew. First, why do we call them kings? The Gospel says the visitors were *magos* in Spanish, that is "magicians," after the Greek *magi,* which described the astrologers of the ancient world. Today we understand them to be "wise men" from the East, that is, perhaps scholars and counselors of the kings of Persia.

Second, why do we assert that there were *three* kings? The Matthew text does not say how many of these visitors there were; presumably the tradition of three wise men arose from the detail that they brought three gifts for the child.

Third, why did they go to Jerusalem if they were following the star? Perhaps they came led by a star until they reached Jerusalem (which was the nearest major city on their route). It seems that they lost faith in the star and went to another source, a human king, to seek help, which alarmed King Herod of Judea, known historically to be wary of challenges to his rule.

Finally, why do we portray the magi at the stable and manger where Jesus was born, when in the Bible they visit the home where the child was living with his parents? The wise men do go to the village of his birth, Bethlehem, but it seems that some time has passed since Jesus was born, and presumably it was an older little boy that they finally celebrated. The shepherds—whom we read about a couple of weeks ago in Luke—were the ones to visit the manger. The wise men visited after a while. (Bible scholars speculate that it may have been as long as two years after Jesus' birth.) In any case, the well-traveled visitors still expressed great joy and adoration at the sight of this child.

Given these more historical questions about the text as given to us, what do we learn today from these wise men's visit to the baby Jesus?

Leadership for the Road

The magi of old were advisers to royalty. We find in our Scripture account that although they are not part of the immediate culture of Jerusalem, they are interested in this newly born "king" of the

Jews, whom even they (as foreigners in the land) acknowledge as a ruler worthy of homage by all peoples. They want to honor him with gifts from their country and culture. We honor our leaders, namely, those who are righteous like Christ, not unrighteous like Herod, who made a plot to eliminate this new king. Unrighteous King Herod ends up murdering children of the presumed age of Jesus, just as Pharaoh did generations earlier, nearly murdering the infant Moses, who would grow up to become Pharaoh's nemesis and the leader of the Hebrew people.

Let us seek righteousness and justice from our political leaders, praying that they be persons who, whether Christian or not, truly care for the well-being of the people they serve and honor as best as they can. Those are the ones we should honor in turn. The wise men were leaders, who came to worship the leader of all leaders, King Jesus.

Light for the Road

At our home every year, it is our daughter, Jasmin, who helps us with the Christmas tree and lights, even though she no longer lives at home. This year Jasmin has been living in New York and was not able to come home till just before Christmas. In addition, Olga was recovering from a knee operation. So the tree-mounting task was mine. I put up the tree and some of the lights. And I put up the outdoors lights, but we had a snowstorm before I finished, and they never got turned on. Jasmin arrived two days before Christmas, and in a matter of minutes the lights outside were turned on, and then we finished the decorations inside. At last we had lights, including the star at the top of the tree! I declared, as I used to say to Jasmin and Joel when they were little, "Now Santa Claus and the three wise men can see to bring the gifts!"

We need our pathways lit up. The wise men had a star that brought them almost to Bethlehem, but they hesitated and went to the mighty, sitting king for help. *He will know where this new king is*, they thought. Well, he wanted to know only in order to kill the competition. Thank God that even with their royal instructions, the wise men finally depended on the star that brought them to the baby Jesus in Bethlehem—and they trusted in the dream that advised them to head home by an alternate route (Matthew 2:12)!

Seek the right lights for your walk with God in the life God has given you. Seek the guidance of the Holy Spirit and those guides in life—pastors and teachers, fathers and mothers, and elders of the church—people who can give good advice, helping to light your way.

Joy on the Road

Finally, the wise men arrived in Bethlehem where the child was, and they had reason for great joy and adoration of the child. They shared their gifts and celebrated with the child's family, praising God for the arrival of a spiritual king, the Savior of the world. They adored him! They worshiped him!

Along our roads of life, there are plenty of difficulties, deviations, sadness, and pain. Yet when we have those moments of "arriving at home," a deep joy transcends all those difficulties, a joy that only God can give. This is why we adore God and worship God. In our walk with Christ, we have joy. We do have dark moments, but the light of God eventually brings us to moments of deep joy. Whenever we come to those places, let us open our hearts with gifts of worship! The church, this special space of worship each Sunday, should be a place of great joy and worship of our God in Christ Jesus.

Conclusion

With this sermon, I officially end my time with you as an interim pastor. I am sure that I will return from time to time to preach. We are brothers and sisters, my friends; you have all entered into my heart and will not come out. In the meantime, I hope that the lessons of the magi—the three wise men—will be ours forever: that in the journey of your life as a church, you seek good *leaders* to lead you well, that you always seek the *light*, the guidance of the Holy Spirit of God, and that all that we do as a church and as individual believers and families may be with great *joy* because we are sons and daughters of God in Christ Jesus now and forever.

Do not forget the teaching of the illustration I shared with you in one of my early sermons: the little girl on the beach who rescued the starfish from drowning even though others told her it was not worth her effort. Do not let anyone near you drown in the problems of life. Be, in the name of Christ, someone who will rescue the vulnerable, and not let other people sink. When you come across people in need, whether it be inside the four walls of this church, in your neighborhood, or wherever this way of life leads you, be like Jesus—somebody who rescues, somebody who saves, someone who loves. Amen!

> **Prayer:** *Dear God, bless my sisters and brothers of Second Baptist Church here in this historic neighborhood of East Harlem, New York. Bless their lives as they seek to choose their next pastor. Help them grow in peace and love, leadership and joy. Give them all they need to serve this church, their families, and their communities. And may the peace of Christ, which surpasses all understanding, and which those traveling magi soon experienced after their long journey, be with them forever. This is my prayer in Christ's name. Amen!*

A Personal Note on This Sermon: One Final Word / As noted at the beginning of the sermon, Three Kings Day on January 6 was another celebration, like Advent, that neither in my religious upbringing nor apparently in Second Spanish Baptist Church was practiced with any regularity. In Boston, by way of contrast, at Hispanic Community Church of Boston (UCC), which Olga and I attended with our children in the early 1990s, the Three Kings Sunday service each year was an entire community event, where Latino/a politicians and community leaders would show up and kids from church families and nonchurch families would receive gifts. The pastors and church leaders would take turns putting on the Three Kings robes, and special music and preaching would celebrate the occasion. It became a moment to celebrate Latino/a culture and faith and to unite the community, church members or not, around our traditions, religious and cultural. The church bore witness to Christ in that way.

So, in my final sermon at Second Spanish Baptist Church of New York, I encouraged the church to continue on its road to God in Christ, with recognition of who they were as a Latino/a church, but also in consideration of their changing surroundings in historic East Harlem. In the annual meeting that followed this service, I reported on my experience, thanking the church for this important opportunity in my life as a Christian, a teacher, and a preacher. I encouraged the congregation to consider ways to meet the challenges as a church moving forward in the early twenty-first century, a changing landscape. What would work best—continuing business as usual, a reconsideration of their Spanish-language dominance as a church, becoming more bilingual instead, or realizing that their changing surroundings included a more Latin American than just Puerto Rican flavor, as well as the ongoing gentrification of the neighborhood with many non-Latinos/as as well? Accepting the challenges I lay before them in these final moments as their interim pastor, they sent Olga and me off with some lovely parting gifts and enthusiastic words of gratitude. I was thankful to them as well, as I still am these several years later.

Epilogue

After several months with supply preaching and an in-depth search for a permanent pastor, Second Spanish Baptist Church of New York secured a new pastor, and he was well-known to them. He had been pastor of a sister church in Brooklyn, which had hosted a minister's meeting that I had attended during my tenure at Second Baptist. He had preached on the church's eighty-fifth anniversary in October 2013 and had done a fine job. He lived in Mount Vernon, New York, so the commute to East Harlem was much easier than to Brooklyn for him and his family. And the church leaders, one of them later reported to me when I asked, felt led by the Spirit as one unified voice to call him as Second Baptist Church's third settled, hopefully long-term pastor in the last fifty years or so.

The choice of this pastor, a Costa Rican immigrant with strong ties to Latin America, signaled a choice, I felt reflecting on it later, in the options that I had presented to the church during my interim tenure. It seems that Second Spanish Baptist Church of New York would continue to be a Spanish-language-dominant church in its primary language for worship and service. However, the days when the Puerto Rican community would dominate the leadership and constituency of this community, both inside and outside the church, were probably behind it. The growing Latin American— Mexican and Central American in particular—presence in East Harlem will be well-served, it seems to me, by a pastor with such a strong Central American background, who, however, has been in this country long enough to know, even with his own children, that bilingualism and biculturalism, which have marked this church for more than eighty-five years, are also part and parcel of what it means to be a Latino/a church in the United States, including in the great city of New York.

Other Lessons

After only eight months as an interim minister, a third experience of doing so in some twenty-five years for me, I became convinced yet again that my service to God and God's community is best exercised in the seminary classroom. While I enjoy the preaching ministry, even on a more consistent basis than occasional supply or guest preaching, pastoral ministry is not just about preaching, especially in the Latinx church. Pastoral care and counseling, careful church administration, church leadership development, community outreach—all of these constitute the twenty-first-century ministry of the US Latino or Latina pastor. The glimpse into this helps me be a better seminary professor, but the ministry itself demands so much more than a part-time pastor, full-time professor can give.

Moreover, given the changing landscape of the mainland Protestant church in particular, which is declining in numbers as never before,[1] the future of the Protestant church perhaps lies in its non-white expressions. Indeed, there are several emerging Latino and Latina pastoral leaders, who with their significant theological education experiences and pastoral experiences in Latinx churches, are impacting mainline, predominately white and multicultural churches, now more than ever. I am thinking about colleagues I know in the Northeast, such as the Reverends Damaris De Leon Whitaker, Persida Rivera-Mendez, and Edwin Ayala in the United Church of Christ, the Reverends Pablo R. Diaz, Victor Aloyo, and Karen Herandez-Granzen in the Presbyterian Church, USA, Rev. Eli Valentin in the American Baptist Churches USA, and Rev. Lydia Lebron-Rivera in the United Methodist Church, to name just a few whom I know personally. These are clergy who have "crossed over" from serving exclusively Latinx churches to more multicultural or majority white churches because the need is there and the

Latino/a pastorate has been well-trained through experience and theological education to cross over culturally, linguistically, and theologically to serve wherever the need is great.

This, too, is a legacy of churches like Second Spanish Baptist Church in East Harlem, which with over eighty-five years of history, long ago started producing rich and successful ministers and servants of the gospel. As mentioned at the outset of this volume, during my tenure at Second Baptist, I was reminded of the rich heritage that came out of this church or was impacted by the ministry of this church. I mentioned my dear colleagues and friends in theological education, Dr. Loida Martell-Otero, who began her tenure as dean at Lexington Theological Seminary in the summer of 2017, and Dr. Elizabeth Conde-Frazier, dean of Esperanza College in Philadelphia. Dr. Conde-Frazier's colleagues in the wider Esperanza U.S.A. ministry, Reverends Luis Cortes and Daniel Cortes, are direct products of La Segunda. I did not mention previously two other products of La Segunda, longtime member Wanda Pazmiño, and her husband, Robert, who came to the church as a doctoral student in the 1970s, where he and Wanda met and married. Years later Bob was a professor of mine at Gordon-Conwell Theological Seminary. He always spoke so highly of his experience at La Segunda that when the church came calling years later, I remembered Bob's high regard for the church. In May 2018, as I was finishing this book, Professor Pazmiño completed his wonderful career as a seminary professor, including close to thirty-five years at his second post, Andover Newton Theological School in Boston.

Indeed, Second Spanish Baptist and Latinx churches all over the country are the "gifts that keep on giving." So more Martell-Oteros, Conde-Fraziers, Cortes brothers, and Pazmiños will follow, just as they followed the likes of well-known Latino Baptist leaders Rev. Francisco Santiago, Rev. Rafael Martell, and Dr. Orlando Costas.

Finally, in one of my sermons in this volume, I mentioned a longtime leader at Second Baptist, deacon for life Viterba Ortiz, who celebrated her one hundredth birthday in September 2016. She has been at La Segunda since the 1940s, some seventy-five years! The future of any Latinx church, as for any Christian church or religious body anywhere, lies in the quality and endurance of its lay leadership. Most folks will not be as active as Sister Viterba at age one hundred (at age ninety-six she was still leading noontime prayer services at the church every Wednesday when I was there in 2013!). However, without quality lay leadership, the church is in trouble. Theological schools and professors, denominational leaders and congregational pastors, and religious educators want to be mindful of that as well moving forward. Thank you, Second Baptist Church and Sister Viterba Ortiz, for these important lessons.

Note
1. See, for example, the 2015 study by Pew Research Center: "Mainline Protestants Make Up Shrinking Number of U.S. Adults," May 18, 2015, http://www.pewresearch.org/fact-tank/2015/05/18/mainline-protestants-make-up-shrinking-number-of-u-s-adults/.